T0197337

Adrift

Completely At Sea With Paranoid Schizophrenia

NICKI ADAMS

authorHOUSE®

AuthorHouse™ UK Ltd.
1663 Liberty Drive
Bloomington, IN 47403 USA
www.authorhouse.co.uk
Phone: 0800.197.4150

Published by AuthorHouse 05/19/2014

ISBN: 978-1-4969-7738-0 (sc)
ISBN: 978-1-4969-7739-7 (hc)
ISBN: 978-1-4969-7740-3 (e)

Library of Congress Control Number: 2014906683

Contents

Introduction

If I had been able to access any recommended reading material to help and support me through the traumatic experiences I endured, obtaining help would have been so much easier. It would also have made me feel more able to cope. At the time, in the late 1970s and early 1980s, it seemed there was little to help me understand the gradual disintegration of my husband's personality. The support services were ineffective, professional help for him sporadic, and guidance for me sadly limited. Feeling terribly isolated and deeply confused, I simply had to follow my best judgement and hope for the best as I dealt with him and his condition of paranoid schizophrenia. It is my sincere wish that this account of events can assist others in some way; for example, I hope this book helps readers understand aspects of mental illness or realize that they are not alone if faced with a similar seemingly insurmountable problem. If this is the case, I also hope that my story helps them to find some strands of comfort in any common threads.

As I write this, almost four decades after this episode in our lives occurred, I am assured that there is now much better provision in the United Kingdom to support sufferers and their families. Each experience is different, and I believe that everyone has a story to tell. With the ever-changing reorganization of support services and increasing financial pressure, I hope that this account serves to demonstrate how important such services are and how easily things can fall apart if public funding is reduced and the management of services for the mentally ill is relaxed.

It has taken all these years for me to decide to recount from my notes the exact sequence of events that destroyed my marriage. The account is written entirely from my own perspective. As well as the obvious recovery period which I needed to come to terms with the emotional trauma and rebuild my own life, I needed to devote the intervening years to bringing up my children, to advancing my professional career, and to living life again, free from the shadows cast by fears from the past. In retrospect, I realize that the eight years I spent with Vincent comprised a relatively short episode of my life. Yet during the period when he was at his most disturbed, it seemed as if I was in the middle of a lifelong commitment with no chance of relief. For those nine months, feeling conflicted and at my wit's end, I endured terrifying attacks of physical and mental abuse, always in the naive hope that Vincent would eventually submit to treatment and that his original personality could be recovered, at least in part.

With hindsight, I understand more clearly how fear, confusion, lack of confidence, ignorance, and uncertainty clouded my vision. The psychological effects of Vincent's aggressive onslaughts had inevitably sown the seeds of self-doubt in my mind, which added to the recovery time that I needed. They also caused me to distance myself from this episode in my life before I could record my reflections as accurately as possible. My sense of inadequacy was compounded by the feeling that I had neglected to challenge my husband more assertively and actively seek support for myself during his illness.

As well as showing how a loving relationship can disintegrate due to mental illness, this true story documents an important part of our family history for our children. In recounting my experiences to various people over the years, it was evident that I could only ever share fragments. The complete story now needs to be told and shared.

To protect the identity of individuals, all names have been changed.

Chapter 1

Aspirations

Life was full to the brim. During the working week, Vincent would look after our son, Andy, while I went out to work at a local school. As soon as I came home, our roles would reverse. I took care of Andy while Vincent continued refurbishing the house in an effort to complete the most pressing building work before the birth of our second baby, due on my birthday, 30 October. Soon I would be able to enjoy the summer looking after Andy full time during the six-week school holidays. He would be two years old in August. Then, after the new baby was born, Vincent and I had jointly agreed that the plan would be for him to return to work and for me to resign from my teaching job.

'Has Andy been sleeping for long?' I asked.

'For about half an hour,' replied Vincent, looking exhausted but relaxed.

I looked through the front window. 'I think there's a storm brewing. Look at the sky!' Outside, dark clouds were gathering. Within a short while the daylight turned almost to night even though it was still only about four o'clock. It resembled a full solar eclipse. Vincent was in the process of replacing the roof at this stage of the building work. Up in the main bedroom, which was being used as a workshop, the house was open to the sky, protected only by sheets of polythene flapping in the breeze.

The house was slowly being transformed into a beautiful family home. A Victorian end-of-terrace house on a busy street in South London, it was situated close to a lovely park where I walked the dogs each day. There were two rooms in the basement which Vincent had already modernized before

I met him in 1974. The rest of the house had been neglected and needed complete modernization. The kitchen on the ground floor at the rear of the house led out to the back garden. The living room had been converted into one large open-plan area with stairs leading to other areas of the house—a few steps down to the kitchen, and a few more to the basement rooms. Another staircase led from the living area up to the bedrooms. The spacious bathroom above the kitchen would soon be luxurious after months of extensive work. At the top of the house, the airy front bedroom and the children's bedroom next to it both awaited renovation.

Thunder and lightning struck and, before we had a chance to gather all manner of receptacles to catch the water, heavy rain started to seep through the gaps between the polythene sheets. Hurriedly we placed buckets, bowls, saucepans, and other assorted vessels in position as the rain came down like stair rods. Meanwhile, down in the basement water was also coming in, threatening to flood the hall and two rooms. It was mayhem.

'Quick, switch the pump on in the kitchen!' ordered Vincent. He had had the foresight to install a heavy-duty pump submerged in a well which had to be dug out deep below the kitchen floor. This was not the first time that the basement had flooded. Apparently an underground river, the River Effra, flowed under the houses on the street exacerbating any flood risk. The water from the pump was channelled to a drain outside. Still the water poured into the house, top and bottom, until the storm subsided. Fortunately, we had very few belongings in the basement rooms, and there were no carpets laid. With the windows and doors open, the flooded area soon dried out, hopefully without lasting damage.

Apart from minor setbacks of this kind we were well on track towards fulfilling our shared dreams, aims, and desires. What Vincent and I shared was a wish to raise a family together, to enjoy the comfort of a lovely home, and to lead a happily married life. Simple enough! So how did it all fall apart? Our life together had started so well.

When we first met in 1974 Vincent was working as a carpenter for a London building firm. I was living in a shared a flat in gentrified Holland Park, the last property in the street to remain in disrepair. I was in my second year of teaching French and German in a tough and very large Inner London comprehensive school. Such was my dedication and enthusiasm that one weekend I actually went into the school to paint the notice boards in my classroom and pin up a stack of pictures, which I had also painted myself. When students in one of my classes asked if I would take them to Paris on a school trip, I thought it would be great fun. I was so green that I even fully expected to pay for my own ticket! Little did I realize how much work was involved in the planning, which was further complicated by the different nationalities of some of the pupils who needed visas. Before the end of my second year at the school my head of department and deputy head of department both left for new jobs without any replacements appointed. I took a share of the management responsibility to run the department on a temporary basis with a fellow colleague.

Both Vincent and I took our work very seriously. Vincent described himself as a master craftsman. His superior skill was evident on my first visit to the house in which he rented the two basement rooms, the same house that we were eventually able to buy. His work was meticulous.

Teaching French and German in those days involved using open-spool tape recorders and slide projectors, which were very heavy and cumbersome pieces of audiovisual equipment. Although much of my time was spent planning lessons and marking homework, I enjoyed partying and meeting friends at the local pub. I was a happy singleton. Borrowing my friend's bicycle for a while, I also enjoyed cycling around the streets. I did my food shopping in Portobello Road market where several new vegetarian cafés were opening. There were also record shops in the area where I could buy second-hand albums or even do swaps. The music scene was rich and exciting. Cream, Roxy Music, David Bowie, and Peter Gabriel offered vibrant home-grown music, while Curtis Mayfield; Isaac Hayes; Neil Young; and Crosby, Stills and Nash provided amazing new sounds from the United States, which I loved.

In addition to the music scene, the other thing which I really liked about living in London was the rich mix of nationalities. This was in stark contrast to my hometown where racial segregation, prejudice, and narrow-minded conventional attitudes still prevailed. The London school where I worked had a very international intake. I felt that I was in my element, as I could not stand racism and enjoyed being immersed in the diverse mix of cultures. Before long I had a boyfriend. Jimmy was a couple of years younger than I. We enjoyed the same taste in music and films. We went to see *Shaft* and *The Harder They Come* at the local cinema in Notting Hill Gate. It was through him that I met Vincent, as they worked in the same place and had made friends with each other. We first met up in a pub near the cinema where they sometimes met for a drink after work.

I was not initially attracted to Vincent. He seemed much older than I. At that time I was twenty-six and he was thirty-four. He described himself as a Scots Jamaican Jew, according to his racial heritage. Like most black men at the time, he had an Afro hairstyle. He was tall and slim and had a beard. Somehow the big hair, rather coarse features, and dusky complexion looked incongruous with the tweed suit he wore. Little did I know at the time that he had once been a fashion model for a short period as was eventually revealed when he showed me a cutting from a London newspaper that had done a feature on him. The picture showed enough of his physique to capture my more immediate interest, revealing his clean-shaven face and toned muscles. The Afro suited him much better without the suit. Without the beard, his facial features were revealed, and the shape of his face with its clearly defined jawline and cheekbones made him look more refined. He had auditioned for the hit musical stage show *Hair*, which I had seen as a student. It did not occur to me that Vincent would find me attractive. Besides, he already had a girlfriend. She was from Ireland but came over frequently to spend weekends with him.

In the prime of my mid twenties, I had long, straight brown hair hanging over my shoulders, and I applied my black eye make-up heavily over my green-blue eyes. I was short sighted so occasionally wore glasses, which were held together with sticky tape. Following the fashion of the day, I wore flared jeans with platform shoes or my crippling yellow leather clogs with their thick wooden soles. I had recently moved to London after completing my degree and teaching qualification. Having lived on a shoestring for five years as a university student, I had never had money for clothes. When I finally did start earning a salary, instead of shopping for clothes, I bought a rusty old car and took driving lessons to get myself through my driving test. One day as I was driving home to the flat, which I shared with friends from my hometown in the Midlands, the wheel actually fell off the car as I came round a corner. 'Crunch!' Fortunately I was able to have it fixed at little cost at a local garage. Social values were still in transition following the 1960s and the hippie movement. Many young people, myself included, showed little interest in consumerism.

What struck me about Vincent from the outset was his stimulating conversation and his strong personality. In some respects he seemed larger than life. His laugh had a wicked kind of resonance. He was articulate and outspoken about most things, always attaching a philosophical commentary to everything. Revealing himself to be a mature man of strong principles and rich life experience, he inspired respect. I also found him to be very generous, considerate, and well mannered.

Accompanied by our respective partners, we went out together a few times for drinks. Then I went on holiday to Italy with Jimmy and a friend of mine who worked as a nanny in the house next door. We took a long train journey all the way down the leg of Italy stopping off at beaches where we slept out under the stars and woke to the sound of the waves lapping the shore. In one coastal village, a young boy called Umberto made friends with us and taught me a few words in Italian. When we arrived in Sicily, it was so insufferably hot that we decided to get straight back on the train and make our way back up the Italian coast. I included Vincent among the friends I sent postcards to.

On our return from Italy, we met up as usual as a group at a club in Hampstead where African drummers often performed. I was still recovering from a slight tummy bug and went outside to linger a while in the fresh air away from the smoky atmosphere. There I heard Vincent calling to me in his resonant voice with a hint of urgency: 'Nicki, Nicki. Are you all right?'

'Just a moment . . . I'm fine.'

It was when I returned to our table that Vincent took me completely by surprise by asking me to dance. Then he whisked me back outside and he kissed me. Could it be that my suntan made me so irresistible, I wondered. Maybe it was my relaxed mood after the holiday. Most probably Vincent had started to kindle feelings for me before I had left for Italy, and the absence had played on his fantasies. Whatever it was, for my part, for the first time, I was forced to look at him in a completely different light. Overwhelmed by his advances and carried away by the romantic moment,

I could not help but feel the stirrings of an intense physical and emotional attraction.

As I still had feelings for Jimmy, I felt quite confused at first. Jimmy had an exuberant personality, but he was young and immature. On reflection I realized that Vincent was a far more serious prospect, being older and much more mature. Before long it was abundantly clear to me that there was absolutely no contest. As my affections transferred, I discovered a depth of feeling for Vincent which strengthened significantly as we planned our future life together.

I had had plenty of boyfriends up to this point in my life. Yet my past romantic relationships had been a bit like adventures rather than the central focus of my life. Moreover, I had travelled very confidently on my own. I had lived and worked abroad: six months in France, six months in Germany, and three months in Sweden. As a student I had explored parts of Spain and Morocco with a boyfriend and another friend. Then, too, we had camped and slept out in the open under the stars. One morning after a night sleeping in a cornfield, we were awakened by the sound of a combine harvester approaching a little too close for comfort. Hurriedly we scuttled out of the field and ran to the car laughing off the dramatic close encounter.

On my return to London I embarked on my teaching career, and my professional life began to take shape successfully. Though I may not have articulated it clearly, my ultimate dream was to settle down, put down roots, and have a family. I had not meticulously planned this out in my mind according to any particular time scale, but, on reflection, this was certainly the prime time in my life for me to enter into a serious relationship, one which could form the foundation for this vaguely envisioned family life.

There was no denying the excitement I felt at the prospect of a sharing my life with Vincent. The physical attraction gathered intensity. When he held me, I felt overawed by his strength. The attraction, growing affection, and respect were mutual. The emotion of the romance overwhelmed us both equally. It did not occur to me to find out about his past or check for references. These were not the rules of the game. We were free agents. We trusted each other. It was a classic case of a couple falling recklessly in love.

We began to see one another as often as possible. Breaking off our previous relationships, we spent each weekend at his rented basement flat, which he had modernized and decorated himself very tastefully. At my shared flat I had little privacy. Now with my own car I could easily drive over to Vincent's in the evenings during the week. He would cook for me or take me for a drive, sometimes out of the city for a quiet drink in a country pub. Sometimes we simply made a love nest in his flat and listened to his superb record collection. We shared the same taste in music. Favourites included albums by Steve Winwood and Traffic, Yes, Led Zeppelin, and Pink Floyd as well as new releases by Bob Marley and the Wailers, which we would play at particularly high volume.

Chapter 2

Contrasts

Before long I moved in with Vincent. I quickly made friends with his fuzzy black cat called Fluff. As a sign of acceptance, she would rub her furry head against my ankles purring wildly and working herself up into a state of near ecstasy. Fluff had a black tomcat friend which belonged to Marcia, the Jamaican woman who lived in the rooms upstairs. We shared with her the dilapidated unheated kitchen and bathroom.

The rented basement consisted of two rooms and a hallway with a smart wooden coal bunker at the front end. Just behind the back basement door was an outside toilet. Vincent had replaced the original flooring with new floorboards, which he had laboriously sanded by hand and coated with clear varnish. He had replaced the panels in the doors with glass to allow light to pass through. The central feature of each of the two rooms was a fireplace.

In the front room, an enclosed multi-fuel stove sat on a hearth of carved York stone. On the mantelpiece above rested a gigantic gold-framed mirror. When fired up with flaming coal, this stove was sufficient to heat both rooms. The next-door neighbour was a coal merchant, so we always had a plentiful stock of top-quality fuel. After living for so long in crummy rented accommodation, I was unaccustomed to living in such tasteful surroundings, though the furnishings in Vincent's flat were sparse. There was only a double mattress on the floor covered with two goatskin-lined coats. Fitted shelving in one alcove formed by the chimney breast provided space for the stereo and record collection. In the other alcove a black angle poise lamp perched like a giant crouching insect on the desk that consisted of a glass surface framed with wood.

In the back room, inside the unused open fireplace the irregular brickwork was painted white and a sturdy distressed wooden beam had been inserted across the top to form a mantelpiece. An illuminated tank of tropical fish set in the fireplace added spectacular colour and life to the room. I marvelled at the intricacy of the work that Vincent had completed in such confined conditions on the other side of the room in the open space under the stairs. He called this 'the cosy'. He had constructed a clothes rail, a long shelf, a chest of drawers with an oval mirror, and two spotlights. Because of my travels and lack of money, I had acquired few possessions. The only belongings I contributed to the household were a stack of books, a few ornamental items, my antique sewing machine, and a few records. We discovered that we both owned a copy of *Third*, the Soft Machine album.

The job of furnishing our basement flat now started in earnest. For the front room we bought a new sofa, a beautiful swivel chair upholstered in faux cream leather, and a brown cowhide rug. We moved the mattress from the front room to the back room, which became our bedroom. Vincent made a large coffee table that was big enough to double as a dining table. The flat, which had seemed bare when I had first moved in, now looked fully furnished and homely.

We decided to sell my old car, as I could drop Vincent to work in his Mini and continue my journey to work in West London, stopping on the way in Pimlico to pick up my colleague Kate from the basement flat where she lived. She was tall and willowy and very good fun. She had a lovely dog who used to lap water from a tall jug on the floor. The walls of the jug seemed to amplify the lapping sound, making the water appear to be extremely appetising. I became good friends with both willowy Kate and her water-lapping dog.

Settled and happy with my new life, I adapted quickly to living with a partner. I felt that I had had enough of travelling and seeking adventure. Besides, getting to know Vincent better was like a whole new adventure in itself. Our personalities complemented each other well. Life with him was fun. We had a social life that included visiting Vincent's friends in the neighbourhood or my friends from work. In addition we received visitors and enjoyed going to parties. We were also just as content to stay home relaxing together and enjoying each other's company. I never grew tired of listening to Vincent talk about his amazing past. He had experienced a lot of emotional hardship as child.

Up to the age of eight he had been brought up in Jamaica by his maternal grandmother while his mother was away working. His grandmother had been a teacher and had kept a store of books for him, which he enjoyed reading. But he did not see much of his mother, who by this time was divorced from his father. When Vincent was eight years old, his father sent for him. Vincent took the opportunity to travel to England to live with his father who shared a house in Beaconsfield with his new family. Travelling alone by ship with a virtual stranger to keep an eye on him must have been very difficult at such a tender age. When he arrived, it was a blow to find that his father was very distant towards him. Apparently he was very strict and had unrealistically high expectations regarding his son. Vincent did not get on at all well with his stepmother, half-sister, or his stepmother's sister, who also lived with them.

By pressuring Vincent, his father had expected that he would develop an interest in maths at school. Never feeling happy living with his father, Vincent failed to live up to his father's expectations. His father had drilled maths into him and forced him to learn how to use a slide rule. However Vincent was far more interested in art, but his father discouraged this. Sometimes Vincent truanted from school and found it difficult to form close friendships. By the end of his schooling he had O-level general certificate of education (GCE) qualifications in several subjects and a special interest in art. First he became an apprentice toolmaker and worked as a mechanic in a local garage. In the meantime, his father left home and moved to the United States, while his half-sister moved to Australia. Without a family or a home base in Beaconsfield, Vincent was left to fend for himself. This must have had a profound impact on him.

Having nowhere to stay, Vincent spent more than one bitterly cold night on a park bench. With no money for fares, he decided to walk all the way to the East End of London, a distance of probably more than forty miles, to look up a family he had once known who might be willing to let him sleep on the floor for a while. Eventually this contact led him to more permanent accommodation with a painter and decorator and his family.

Regarding this man as a master in his trade and acting as his apprentice, Vincent acquired many useful skills. It was while he was working with him and living with his family that he married the daughter who was training to work as a midwife. He always referred to this as a marriage of convenience. Taking into account his insecure upbringing and the hostility shown by his father and other family members, this is not difficult to understand.

While his new wife was completing her professional training, Vincent's interest turned to music. He formed a band, which proved to be popular, and so, on tour around the country, he travelled further and further away from home. The band became more and more successful and was booked for university gigs. For a while they were the resident band at the Playboy Club in London. As well as managing the band, doing all the driving, and maintaining the van, Vincent worked professionally as a singer, writer, and musical arranger. Unfortunately, it was when the band was on the brink of commercial success, with their first record planned, that the band split up. The reasons he gave for the split-up included a lack of total commitment by the band members, which led to their lack of reliability, and the underhand dealings going on in the music industry. This was an exciting time for music in the 1960s. The Beatles were at their peak of popularity and were beginning to incorporate Eastern elements into their music.

Following this, Vincent worked for a short time as a model and moved to South London. At the time he was among the first black models, which prompted publicity that predicted the certain success of 'Wide-eyed Vincent' according to one newspaper article he showed me. In addition to the selection of newspaper cuttings, he kept a collection of photos of himself posing in elegant clothes of the period alongside beautiful female models. Unable to tolerate what he found to be the artificial and superficial world of fashion, he abandoned this career and moved to the basement flat in the house which we now occupied together. For a spell he tried his hand at fashion photography, again showing evidence of this in his collection of professional fashion photographs featuring April, who was to become his second wife. She was tall, slim, and attractive. However, as she had returned to her native country, Canada, after the break-up of their marriage, I never had the opportunity to meet her. I was curious about their relationship and in particular the reasons for their break-up.

Apparently they had been very close and deeply in love with each other. After leading a bohemian lifestyle with neither of them working for a while, eventually, out of necessity, Vincent took a few local jobs painting and decorating just to earn some money. Although he excelled at this, he decided to specialize in carpentry and to work for a firm, preferring the security of a regular income.

April took a job at a local department store in the cosmetics department. It was then that Vincent claimed they started to drift apart. He felt that she became influenced by the friends she had made at work, an idea that she disputed. This, he told me, had led to violent arguments. On one occasion, she decided to leave him and went to stay with a friend. Although he persuaded her to come back, soon the arguments started up again. One day Vincent came home to find that April had taken her belongings and left, this time for good. As a result, Vincent cut himself off from all contact with people for a few months until he felt ready to face the world again. The break-up had obviously wounded him deeply. However, without her testimony, it was impossible for anyone to assess who was to blame or exactly what had happened.

She left behind a bundle of jewellery, some Christmas decorations, and her heavy winter coat, which, with Vincent's approval, I adopted as my own. I particularly liked the big furry collar and enormous pockets. I asked if he or April had ever been in contact since she left. Although she had once written to Vincent, simply asking how he was, he did not bother to reply. Judging by his expression, it was clear that he had recovered from the rift and had become resigned to starting afresh.

Enter wife number three. Me. Trusting by nature, I accepted Vincent's descriptions of his former marriages as well as everything else he told me about his past life. In stark contrast, my own past life seemed pretty tame. I had had the benefit of a very secure upbringing with two working parents and a sister only seventeen months older than myself, so we were close as children. My family were never lavish with their affection, but we knew we were loved and cared for. At that time, it was quite normal to grow up in a house without central heating, fridge, or phone. But we always had food on the table, coal for the fire, a television, and a car. I had the privilege of a high school education, holidays abroad, grandparents, and heaps of aunts, uncles, and cousins all growing up together and living within easy travelling distance. I had worked hard at school but without ever feeling pressured by my parents. It had been entirely my own decision to study modern languages at university and to become a teacher.

Life for my grandparents must have been much harder. My maternal grandfather had worked as a coal miner. Bits of coal were visible under the skin on his hands. He had a huge beer belly from heavy drinking. My mother used to tell us how he would come home drunk, beat up my grandmother, and turn all the children out of their beds. Because of this, all his children and grandchildren despised him, even though he would give us three pence for sweets each week when we visited. My paternal grandparents had led a less dramatic life but no less difficult. My grandpa, a meek and mild-mannered man, had contracted a lung condition from the dusty atmosphere of working in the potteries and had been a prisoner of war in a Japanese camp. For as long as I remember he had a persistent, dry cough that boomed, resounding in his chest, as he told us stories which, for some strange reason, always ended with, 'And the rain came down in torrents.' They usually gave my sister and me a bar of chocolate whenever we visited.

Books did not feature prominently at home during our years at primary school, apart from the stories of Beatrix Potter and Enid Blyton borrowed from the local library and my own copies of *Alice in Wonderland* and the Bible, which, among the illustrations, even featured a picture of God. The musical soundtrack of our early teenage years was dominated by the Beatles, but we had little money for records and so relied heavily on pirate radio stations. Our leisure time was occupied by television, bike rides, village hall dances, youth clubs, pen friends, boyfriends, and waiting for the 172 bus. In our mid to late teenage years, we continued to follow the exciting music scene, when American soul music provided the soundtrack, including Tamla Motown (Motown's foreign label) as well as classic gems from Otis Reading and James Brown. When I was in the sixth form, my homework took up most of my free time, but once or twice a week I became a regular at the only nightclub in town where I enjoyed dancing until it was time to catch the last bus home. Our parents never ferried us to and fro by car, so if we missed the last bus home we would have to walk the two miles home from town and face a stiff telling off, as we did not have keys. When my sister got married and her young husband moved in with us for a while, I had to move into the single bedroom where, to the annoyance of my parents, I pinned up a picture of Jimi Hendrix on the wall.

We were fortunate that our lives had not been disrupted by war as the young lives of our grandparents and parents had been. After leaving school, our mother had worked in an ammunitions factory. Our father had been a pilot in the Royal Air Force for the duration of the Second World War. He had then worked as a toolmaker and finally as a planning engineer for the National Coal Board. In spite of his professional status, our family identified itself essentially with the working class. Resistant to the notion of social class, if I had to categorise myself at all, I preferred to regard myself as belonging to the educated class, without denying my working class roots.

Not too long after my sister and I left home to make our way in the world as young adults, the family house suddenly acquired central heating, a fridge, and eventually a phone. Following the family tradition, my sister, who had got married when she was about nineteen, settled down to raise a family in our hometown. At the point when I left for university our lives took quite different directions. Still with no reliance on a phone, we would keep in touch by means of occasional letters. I was fortunate that my generation was the first in the family to benefit from a university education.

I could never imagine breaking off complete contact with my family as Vincent had done with his. Even though I may not have seen them very often, I knew they were always there if or when I needed them. Hearing about Vincent's past life made me realize how much I had taken my upbringing and family life for granted. Knowing that I could not possibly make up for all the sorrow in his past, I nevertheless felt confident that I would never disappoint him and that we could make a success of our life together. We wanted to be everything to one another. Vincent was very protective towards me, paying me compliments and praising me in front of other people, which made me feel slightly uneasy. The early conditioning I had had in my family tended to exclude demonstrations of effusive emotions towards others, which seemed to be a particularly northern trait. As Midlanders, we were regarded by northerners as southerners, and by southerners as northerners. My parents' home was right in the centre of the country in South Derbyshire very close to the boundary with East Staffordshire and not far from the boundary with Leicestershire.

Vincent's closest friends hailed from Jamaica but had come to the UK at some stage in their adult lives. Whereas they spoke with a strong Jamaican accent, which I found unfathomable, Vincent spoke like a Londoner but had no difficulty understanding the Jamaican accent. Since moving to this flat in South London, he had had a tough time establishing himself within the close-knit Jamaican community. The flat was situated on the border of Herne Hill and Brixton. When he first moved in, the flat had been used as a gambling den for the locals. Vincent was proud of the way he had asserted himself to 'sort them all out one by one' and had subsequently gained their respect. He certainly had a way of challenging people and confronting them with the naked truth of the matter when in dispute. His forceful way with words helped in averting any physical violence. As a peacemaker myself, always keen to appease without confrontation, I admired his courage in facing up to people in this way. According to Vincent, however, there were occasions when he had to resort to verbal threats and found it difficult to contain his anger when dealing with the most truculent individuals. He was very much his own man, never one to be intimidated.

Taking his responsibilities very seriously and remaining true to his principles, Vincent had been careful not to father any children with either of his former wives. He knew his own mind and had very clear ambitions. He wanted to marry a woman who shared his interests. He wanted a home of his own, believing that the home would provide a secure refuge from the pressures of the outside world. He had always wanted a family of three children. Fully intending to live to a ripe old age, he enjoyed the idea of planning for his later years. As these ambitions were compatible with my own less clearly articulated plans, I felt that we were well matched.

Chapter 3

Friendships, Family, and Four-legged Friends

We were not yet in a position to start a family. As we each had a steady income, we were soon able to replace Vincent's old Mini with a later model, a bright yellow one. We enjoyed going out in the evenings regularly, sometimes for drinks, to see friends and to watch the latest films at the cinema. These included new blockbuster movies such as *Jaws*, *Star Wars*, and *The Exorcist*. Around the time of the cinema release of *Enter the Dragon*, starring Bruce Lee, Vincent developed an interest in the wave of martial arts films that were also on release for the first time at local cinemas in the 1970s.

After our first year together, I changed my job, moving to a school in South London closer to home and taking on responsibility as second in charge of the languages department. Vincent and I celebrated our first year together and my new job by throwing a party at the flat. It turned out to be a huge success and helped me to get to know my new colleagues on a more personal level. I had gradually lost contact with the friends I had made at my first school, partly because Vincent felt ill at ease in their company. His main complaint was that he found them pretentious. Respecting his wishes, I was quite willing for us to mix more with friends of his choice from his workplace. This was not a contentious matter, as I had not formed any close attachments with any of my colleagues, apart from willowy Kate who had now left London to live in the Netherlands.

Living close to Brixton as we did, we were invited to lots of blues parties. These were house parties for the Jamaican community, and they often ran late into the night. Rooms were cleared of furniture to make space for pulsating crowds and massive sound systems with gigantic reverberating speakers pounding the base. In the kitchen cans of chilled beer were handed out, and heaped helpings of curried goat with rice and peas were served up on paper plates. The music was the best Jamaican reggae, which I loved. It just took hold of my body making it impossible to stand still. The air was always heavy with cannabis smoke. Many times after a few puffs on a joint, my ears would start singing, I would break into a sweat, and before I knew it I would pass out. Vincent would carry me outside to get some fresh air, which brought me round. He must have been much more resistant to the atmosphere. He no longer smoked weed, which he had formerly smoked heavily, as he had kicked the habit long before I met him. He still smoked cigarettes though. It was the era of vibrant rebel music from which emerged dub reggae and a host of great Jamaican bands. In stark contrast, Marcia, who lived in the flat upstairs would retaliate by playing endless droning songs by her favourite singer, Jim Reeves, which was the polar opposite to our musical taste. It was a case of live and let live.

Vincent associated a lot at work with a young painter called Nigel, who also shared our taste in music. Like me, he was white. A Londoner in his early twenties, he looked up to Vincent as an elder brother. While I was busy keeping pace with ever-increasing amounts of schoolwork, Vincent and Nigel would often go out together to local pubs. Sometimes I was invited to go along with them, but I did not often feel like going out to pubs. Besides, I did not find Nigel to be stimulating company. I sometimes wondered what Vincent gained from their friendship. Nigel seemed harmless enough—a quiet type—but came across as impressionable, showing little drive or initiative, and he was not very bright. Whereas Vincent treated him like a kid brother, Nigel seemed to regard Vincent as his personal guru.

Before long we could afford to change the yellow Mini for a newer smarter model, this time in a deep shade of purple called 'black tulip'. Vincent decided to replace the engine, working through the night to finish fitting a brand new one. We then decided to drive to Cornwall for a week's holiday. We rented a house in Bodmin. This was to be our first holiday together. Vincent invited Nigel to join us. Each day we enjoyed touring to different coastal locations and exploring the landscape. While we were away, Marcia looked after the cat for us.

A short while after we returned from our holiday, Marcia was taken ill and had to spend some time in hospital. As well as returning the favour by looking after her cat, we decided to adopt a young Siamese stray. She was beautiful with creamy coloured fur, brown ears and tail, and bright blue eyes. She was very affectionate and particularly liked to jump on my shoulders to snuggle by my neck. We called her Suki, probably the most common choice of name for a Siamese cat, but it suited her perfectly. Her presence affected Fluff instantly, who felt that her territory had been rudely invaded. So Fluff, who already preferred living outdoors, lived out the rest of her days outside in the garden, while Suki ruled the roost in the comfort of the flat.

At my new school, I had begun to get to know one my colleagues. Carol Webb was American and taught history. When once we sat together on a coach for a school history trip to St Albans, we had time to chat at greater length.

'Where in the UK have you travelled?' I asked.

'Derbyshire,' she replied, which sounded odd with her American accent.

'I'm from Derbyshire,' I added. 'Where exactly have you visited?'

'My husband is from a small town near Burton-on-Trent,' she continued.

'That's a coincidence!' I exclaimed, surprised. 'Which small town is your husband from?'

'Swad,' she said to my absolute amazement, as only the locals referred to Swadlincote as Swad, which is pronounced 'Swod'.

'That's incredible! I went to school in Swad. What's your husband's name?'

'Ray.'

'My goodness! Surely not Ray Webb! Is he tall and thin and about my age?'

'I guess you could say so. Gee. Do you mean to say that you know him?'

'Yeah. Isn't that amazing! If he's the Ray Webb I remember, we went to the same school and were even in the same class. Ask him if he remembers me. We'll have to meet up and check each other out.'

So we arranged to meet up the following week at our flat. The suspense was over the moment Ray walked in. He was indeed the same Ray whom I remembered as a nine-year-old. As a boy he was always hyperactive. With his long legs and the association with a spider's web because of his surname I had always thought of him as spidery character. Now he was over six feet tall, energetic and, if anything, even more spidery than ever. He worked as a professional artist, which was of particular interest to Vincent and me. After reminiscing about primary school and our home territory, we arranged to visit Ray and Carol at their home to look at some of Ray's artwork. This was followed by several meetings together for drinks and a further meeting our flat.

'I like your rug. What animal is it from? Does it bite?' asked Carol.

'Don't worry. It's only the remains of our last visitor,' joked Vincent, who enjoyed putting visitors on edge with his black humour. We talked about our plans to buy the house at some stage in the future.

'How many bedrooms are there?' asked Ray.

'Two on the top floor and then these two in the basement, which can be used as bedrooms as well,' replied Vincent.

'That way we can have a bedroom for each of our pets,' I replied laughing as Suki climbed up on my knee to be stroked.

However, on one embarrassing evening Carol and Vincent, who had each drunk far too much, started arguing and hurling insults at each other using the most abusive language. After that, spidery Ray and I had no more contact with each other until several years later, and my relationship with Carol at work reverted to a strictly professional one.

Two years after I had moved in with Vincent, the opportunity suddenly arose for us to buy the whole house, though the circumstances were very sad. It turned out that Marcia had developed leukaemia. Tragically, she died, leaving two small daughters to be looked after by relatives. The rooms upstairs were vacated, and we put an offer in to the landlord to purchase the house, which was accepted. The house had been neglected for years and needed structural work and complete modernization. Vincent knew exactly what work needed to be done and showed great enthusiasm at the prospect of putting into practice his ideas to transform the house into a family home.

Along with the decision to buy the house, we decided to get married. On the hottest day in the long hot summer of 1976 we tied the knot at our local registry office. In attendance as witnesses were a couple of Vincent's workmates in their work overalls and my friend, willowy Kate, who was in London visiting from the Netherlands. Vincent chose for me a very pretty second-hand ring of white gold. Inside was engraved the word *Lucky*, which at the time seemed more than appropriate, as I felt as if I had been blessed. We celebrated long into the hot night with a party. It seemed inappropriate to stand on formal ceremony since we had already been living together for two years. Besides we needed to devote all our savings to the work on the house. We invited a few friends including some of my sixth form students.

No family members were invited. Vincent had long lost contact with all members of his family. I was no longer in contact with my parents at the time, as they had not been able to come to terms with the fact that I was living with and about to marry a 'coloured man'. Not wanting to put my sister in an awkward position, I decided not to invite her and her family. I was unsure how she felt about Vincent and me. The wedding party was a very informal affair with loud music and merry making. It was held in the house, which we had just bought, having completed the purchase two days before the wedding date. Vincent's friend made jerk pork and hot spicy chicken to serve to our guests. Vincent had so much to drink at the party that he fell fast asleep outside in the back yard, spending our wedding night in the cool night air. How romantic!

My sister had visited us with her husband and two young children a few months before the wedding date. At the time I resented the fact that she had disclosed to my parents the fact that Vincent was black before I felt ready to tell them myself. Either way there would have been no easy way to break the news to them, and I soon overcame my resentment. The stony silence between my parents and me lasted for over two years.

Our life together continued to flourish. When my head of department left the school, I applied for the post and was successfully promoted to this position of management responsibility, which boosted my earnings. Vincent was very settled in his job as a carpenter.

The next addition to the family was a real character. We decided to get a puppy. One of Vincent's workmates had recommended English bull terriers as a family-friendly breed. When we went to look at a litter, we both fell for the runt, the only white puppy with a clearly defined patch over his eye. When we picked him up, the little bundle felt soft and warm and breathed with a slight wheeze. He was absolutely adorable. We called him Bullet. He looked so comical with his tucks and folds and wrinkled frown that passers-by in the street would simply laugh out loud at the sight of him. The folds of flesh where his legs joined his torso made him resemble a baby rhinoceros. Bullet joined the family at the start of my six-week summer holiday so that I could give him lots of attention. He was incredibly destructive whenever he was left alone. While he had Suki for company, she still ruled the roost.

As he grew bigger, Bullet's floppy ears hesitantly stood erect, and he soon developed into a sturdy, chunky animal with a very placid temperament, though to those who did not know him, he was an awesome sight. Now that he was fully grown, he struck most passers-by with fear. They kept a wide berth as they passed us on a narrow pavement, often walking right out into the road with little regard for oncoming traffic. Once in the park a youth on roller skates nervously asked, 'Does your dog bite?'

Vincent replied sardonically, 'You're all right. You've not got enough meat on your legs.'

I was sure that Bullet had a sense of humour too. He would love being rescued from the most impossible situations. For example, outside the back door beside a flight of steps leading up to the yard there was a ledge just wide enough for him to stand on. He would venture on to this ledge somewhat like a mountain goat only then to freeze, as he could not get into reverse gear for fear of falling. And so he would wait there perfectly still until I came to his rescue. Taking him down in my arms, I could only just manage his weight as he grew to full size. If I had my sewing machine out on the coffee table, sometimes he would place his front paws on the table while his hind paws were on the sofa. In this position, he would inadvertently push the heavy sewing machine forward with his weight until it was teetering on the brink. He would need to be rescued again before calamity struck. Yet another trick in his repertoire was to lie under a chair in such a way that, when he stood up, he would walk half way across the room balancing the chair on his back. Once he got his head stuck between some metal fence railings. No amount of manoeuvring him would free him. Vincent had to apply all his strength to actually bend the railings to get him out.

Bullet loved sitting in the front passenger seat of our Mini. If I pushed him onto the back seat when I offered someone a lift, he would climb right back in the front and sit on the passenger's knee, wedged in position with his head pressed hard against the windscreen. The name Bullet suited him well, as he could run incredibly fast, sometimes too fast for his own legs. When, quite out of the blue, an energy spurt seized him, he would charge at top speed like a missile from the front of the hall skidding along the floor as he turned and ran through to the back of the kitchen. Then he would turn again and zoom back and forth. If you stood in his way and he skimmed the back of your knees, you risked your legs collapsing beneath you, causing you to fall headlong to the floor. Before he fell asleep he would let out a long, long sigh and tuck his nose under his paws to keep it warm. Then, when in a deep sleep, he would appear to be stirred by dreams that made him twitch, and he would make funny little yapping noises.

I loved the companionship of our pets. They were so affectionate and made home feel so much more homely. I really enjoyed taking Bullet for his daily walk in the park. As Vincent had now started work on the house, it was usually my responsibility to take the dog out, although Vincent had been keen to help train him as a young puppy. Nigel was also on hand to help with the work on the house. Vincent offered him the use of the two adjoining rooms on the ground floor as living accommodation in exchange for his help. The mutual advantages of this were self-evident. Although I was not keen to have Nigel as a lodger, I did not feel I had grounds to object, as Vincent needed the help, and Nigel was better able to provide it than I.

Nigel was soon able to afford to buy himself a motorbike, and not long after that he replaced it with a sports car. Vincent gave him driving lessons. Although he felt that Nigel would benefit from learning new building skills through his involvement in the work on the house, his teaching methods left a lot to be desired, and Nigel proved to be a poor apprentice. With his slothful movements and subservient nature, he was easy prey for Vincent's sharp criticism whenever things went wrong. Always the perfectionist, Vincent insisted on the highest standards and failed to appreciate the limits of Nigel's capabilities. In his frustration there were times when he felt that Nigel was deliberately attempting to cause him aggravation, whereas, from my perspective, this was far from the truth.

The first main task was to install central heating throughout the house. The pair worked long hours in the evenings after work and every weekend. With my extra work responsibilities as head of department came the need to work long hours at home too. Before long we had saved enough money to buy appliances and materials for the new kitchen. Once the central heating was completed, work began on the kitchen. The old sash window was to be replaced with a completely different shape and size. The old doorway was to be bricked up and an opening made in the adjacent wall for the new doorway. The wall between the kitchen and the landing was knocked out to create an open plan space with stairs leading up to the living rooms and leading down to the basement allowing daylight to fill these spaces. The kitchen floorboards were to be taken up and replaced to match the varnished new wooden floor in the basement. When all this work had been completed, Vincent built fitted cupboards, a set of drawers, and a strong work surface covered with black laminate and edged with hardwood trim. The new sink unit, gas hob, and electric double oven were fitted in place as well as an extractor hood and waste disposal unit. Incredible! I was to live in luxury beyond my wildest dreams by the time all this work was completed. And this was just the kitchen!

Vincent grew totally absorbed in all this work, driving himself hard to complete each stage, but never at the expense of a top-quality finish. The boiler for the central heating system was housed in the original kitchen fireplace surround, which had been opened up to reveal the irregular brickwork and create an interesting feature. Sometimes he would work all through the night with Nigel always patiently on hand. Vincent would turn his hand to everything: plastering, bricklaying, plumbing, glazing, wiring, and tiling. When he lacked skills or experience, he would wrestle with the task until he had mastered it. I used to feel so privileged to be able to go to bed or relax in the warmth of the basement, leaving Vincent and Nigel to struggle on in frosty, cold conditions. Apart from scraping off pitiful quantities of old wallpaper and painting occasional bits of undercoat, I was relegated to making coffee, sweeping up, fetching tools, and ordering materials. On the other hand, I was earning a good salary to help cover the expenses.

When the work on the kitchen had been completed I felt thrilled to potter about, cooking and adding finishing touches to make it feel homely. The sunlight would stream through the glass panel of the new back door, highlighting the natural beauty of the wooden floor and cabinets. I thought how impressed my parents would be if they could only see the high standard of Vincent's craftsmanship.

Some time after our wedding, my sister invited us to spend a weekend with her and her family. While we were there, I took the opportunity to break the ice with my parents and pay them a visit so that I could introduce Vincent to them. He now looked very respectable with his short hair and clean-shaven face, so I expected that his appearance might score him some points. My mother had already started to come to terms with the fact that we were now happily married, and she had resumed contact by letter and telephone. My father took a while longer, but eventually accepted the situation. During our visit, the atmosphere seemed less strained than I had expected, and I let Vincent do a lot of the talking, which was mostly about his plans to further develop the house. I was anxious for Mum and Dad to get to know him and to judge him on his personality, hoping that in the process they would overcome their racial prejudice.

On the surface, the visit had seemed to be successful. Home improvement was a topic that my parents always found very interesting. They had had their own detached house built in 1956 based on a design from the Ideal Home Exhibition and had always enjoyed telling people all about the stages of its construction. It therefore came as an unpleasant surprise after our visit to discover that they had found Vincent to be boastful and overconfident and that they disliked him. They also suspected that he was 'using me'.

Naturally I was disappointed, realizing how deeply engrained their prejudice was and how little regard they had for my happiness. I felt reluctant to visit them again, though Vincent encouraged me to do so on my own, which in time I did. We kept in contact by telephone, and eventually at least Mum came to accept that I was happy with my life. This was important to me, as I knew she could be fretful if anything worried her unduly. She had suffered from postnatal depression and, although going out to work had been much better for her than staying home as a full-time housewife, any work-related stress would easily reduce her to tears. My parents had a very successful marriage, as did my sister. I felt fortunate in this respect and had every expectation that my own marriage would follow a similar course.

Two years after we had bought Bullet, we bought a second puppy, Bailey, a female English bull terrier. She was also white with a brown patch over one ear. By this time Fluff, the cat, had died of old age. Suki still maintained her superior position of authority, keeping the dogs in check by scratching them on the nose if they were disrespectful towards her. Only when it was feeding time did the pecking order change. Then Bullet would assert his authority as the ultimate dominant force. Feeding the animals was a task that demanded extreme care and attention. Bullet would growl if anyone approached his dish, and he would demolish its contents within seconds like a vacuum cleaner. However, whenever at the end of our meal he was offered a savoury morsel on the end of a fork, he was able to exercise great restraint as he daintily transferred the food from the fork to his mouth. Then it was as if he was a completely different animal. We had carefully planned that, when Bailey was two years old, we would start a family—I mean a human one. By then both dogs would be sufficiently grown up before our first-born came along.

My first pregnancy developed smoothly without incident. I continued working until about the end of June. After starting my maternity leave, I still kept busy at home. Heavily pregnant, I managed to reupholster our sofa by getting into odd positions or lying flat on my back to fix the fabric in place. When my due date approached, I attended my last antenatal appointment at the hospital. By sheer coincidence, that was when I started to go into labour. A scan showed that the placenta was in a risky position, so I was admitted straight away for observation, and the baby was finally induced. Vincent visited but appeared to look exhausted and stressed. One of Vincent's colleagues visited with a gift for the baby. It was a soft toy—a cute rabbit with floppy ears. I had to stay in hospital for about a week after the birth as the baby needed photo-therapy treatment. Apparently the combination of my blood group and Vincent's prompted a jaundiced reaction in the baby, but it was not considered to be serious, and the treatment was effective.

For the first few weeks, Andy cried a lot and very loudly. Sometimes he would get in such a state when he cried that I feared he would burst a blood vessel. I was amazed that such a small baby could create such volume. Carrying him close to me in the baby sling helped to reassure and calm him. Vincent had a good way of holding him firmly and confidently in his large hands. Soon we established a structured routine, and life with our newborn settled down. Vincent enjoyed sharing the nappy changing and bath time. Andy responded well to him, and it was good to see them creating a strong bond.

A few months after Andy was born, my sister came to visit. We bought an inexpensive sofa bed, which consisted of two slabs of upholstered foam with a sausage-shaped piece of foam as a backrest. Eventually when Andy was about one year old, my mother also came to visit. It was lovely to see how she bonded with her new grandson. I had been sending them photos of him at regular intervals. At last my sister and mother could now also see the top quality work on the house and appreciate Vincent's strenuous efforts.

Chapter 4

Anxieties Begin to Take Root

We settled into a routine. Vincent would watch Andy while I was at work. I would take over taking care of Andy on my return home. On one day in April as I was trundling on my way home from the park as usual with Andy in the pushchair and one dog on each side, I noticed a strange stillness in the street. There was no traffic, and there were hardly any people around. It was eerily quiet until I walked towards the bend in the road where I suddenly encountered a huge crowd of young men walking menacingly in the middle of the road carrying bricks and sticks. We scurried home quickly to the news that violent protests had broken out in the streets of Brixton following some kind of racist incident. Once I had reached home, I felt perfectly safe. It helped that Vincent was strong and protective and that he was known in the community. Yet now it seemed that life in our home was like living in a bubble well away from any trouble in the outside world.

'Look,' called Vincent from the upstairs back bedroom. 'It looks like a building has been set alight in one of the back streets.'

'Why are there so many police vans waiting across the road?' I asked looking through the front window. It was slightly unsettling to realize that they were lying in wait on the fringes of the troubled areas, and that this was all happening in our own neighbourhood. This was the start of the Brixton riots. Completely unaware of what was about to happen, I had only moments before walked through the streets with our eight-month-old baby!

As the neighbourhood returned to normal after the riots, I resumed my routine, whisking Andy and the dogs out of the house each afternoon as soon as I arrived home from work. This proved to be quite a handful with two strong dogs tugging on their leads as I attempted to keep the pushchair on course. At times I struggled to keep control in the park. Bullet liked to wander off and would sometimes slip through the gate that led into the flower garden, promptly followed by Bailey, while Andy chuckled at their mischievous ways. If I failed to get the dogs back on their leads before they came out of the flower garden, they would often head straight for the public toilets with me in farcical pursuit. By contrast, Vincent was able to maintain a masterful control over them using little more than his tone of voice, but he considered taking them out to be a chore.

At weekends I enjoyed looking after Andy. Sometimes as I was busily clearing up in the kitchen he would grip the tray of his high chair with both hands and rock himself from side to side until he fell asleep. He enjoyed listening to me read stories to him and never tired of Babar the Elephant. Most of the time he seemed content to play while I attended to domestic chores. As soon as he progressed from shuffling on his bottom to walking, he enjoyed loading his wooden truck and pushing it around the room. Sometimes I helped Vincent by cleaning up, as the building work created an enormous amount of dust. Once when I was mopping the floor, Andy was keeping me company by walking round and round in circles. Then he practised walking backwards without looking behind. As he stepped steadily backwards unaware of the bucket of water behind him, I watched him, wondering if he would stumble. With the back of his legs meeting the edge of the bucket he hesitated for a moment as if in slow motion before landing bottom first right in the bucket with a splash. If only I could have caught that moment on film! We laughed till our faces hurt.

What was I doing back at my parents' house in my hometown in the Midlands? With an awful feeling of panic and bewilderment, I looked out of the bedroom window. Where was our car? How did I get here? And why was Vincent not here? How could I contact him? Desperate attempts to speak to him on the public telephone near my parents' house came to no avail. I woke with a jolt.

It was that bad dream again. It was so vivid and disturbing. The dream left me with a vague image of him living in a gloomy bedsitter somewhere in London. It took some time before the reality sunk in that Vincent was right there beside me asleep in our bed. It felt almost as if, for a moment, I had lost my memory of the intervening years since I had left my parents' home more than ten years previously. Then the changes and events of the last few years overwhelmed me with a deep sense of relief: a beautiful home of our own in London, which had been almost completely renovated; an adorable baby son; two lovely dogs and a cat; a secure teaching job; and a devoted husband. It was now the late spring of 1981, seven years after Vincent and I had first met.

Each time I would shrug off this recurring dream without any serious consideration for its associated emotions of utter confusion, disorientation, and separation as if there was a vast ocean between Vincent and me. Once awake I would simply plunge headlong into the daily routine. I had our baby son to attend to, two energetic dogs to feed and walk, and a clingy Siamese cat always starved of affection. A tank full of tropical fish completed the family menagerie. With a full-time teaching job, I already had my hands pretty full. I was much too busy to dwell on such recurring dreams and ponder over their possible significance.

On one occasion when I mentioned to Vincent the recurring dream and the strange brief effect it always had on me, he had no comment to make about it. I was not inclined to believe in things of a mystical nature. I was a pragmatist. My belief system was very soundly based on scientific evidence. Even my degree qualification in modern languages was awarded as a bachelor of science. This included a wide range of ancillary technical subjects to prepare graduates for a career as translator or interpreter. Nevertheless the dream prompted me to wonder if maybe the associated emotion was significant in some way, perhaps symbolic of a problem in communication or some psychological phenomenon. It certainly suggested a troubled subconscious, yet there did not appear to be anything preoccupying my mind. As usual, once I was immersed in my daily routine, the dream faded away.

That morning I crept downstairs to let the dogs out. I made my coffee and went down to the empty basement to open the curtains and feed the fish. I took the nappies out of the drier and carried them up to the lovely spacious new airing cupboard in the bathroom. Then it was time to wash and dress to be ready for my busy day at school. Meanwhile, Andy had woken up and was trying to climb out of his cot. I had to coax him to stay there until I left. Vincent's day started slowly. He was still asleep, as his activities only started after I had left the house. Reluctantly I hastily kissed Andy goodbye. I always missed him when I left for work. Sometimes he was tearful, and I wished Vincent would get up sooner to attend to him. Yet I realized how tired he must still be. Each afternoon when I came home from school to take over the task of looking after Andy, Vincent started his working day to continue the renovations on the house.

Room by room this work was beginning to feel like an endless slog. At least the major structural work of renewing the roof was now finished, and the decorating of our bedroom was almost complete. Having made the bed frame himself, Vincent was in the process of making two bedside tables. He was beginning to show some annoyance towards me, making accusations that I failed to appreciate the effort that he made or take any real interest in the work. To be honest, I would have been happier to buy a bed and bedside tables rather than face such accusations. It had been his own wish to make the furniture himself. I realized that it must have taken a lot out of him to replace the roof more or less single-handed with only me to help. I had turned my hand quite well to cutting slate roof tiles and enjoyed acquiring many other practical skills to help out as best as I could. It had been about three years since Nigel had left. As Andy still needed to be looked after, it had been difficult for me to be of much more assistance, though I much preferred helping out and being actively involved in the work to standing around simply watching.

We had agreed that, once Andy was four months old, I would stop breastfeeding and return to full-time teaching. It was a workable arrangement for Vincent to look after him while I was out during the day. This way the house could be completed without the pressure of Vincent also having to go out to work. He was now forty and had developed trouble with his back, a recurring problem. It was particularly painful if he had to do a lot of heavy lifting or bending. Obviously much of the work still to be done involved strain on his back. Having already pushed his body to its limit, and sometimes beyond, it was important for him to pace himself and work a more reasonable schedule. His back was checked by the doctor but treatment options were limited. The main priority was to avoid further damage.

We had also planned for sharing childcare between us in this way to continue until the time came when I would have to sop work due to my second pregnancy. Once Vincent had then found a new job, I hoped that I could take a break from teaching and look after the children until they were old enough to start school. Though we could not be certain that everything would go according to plan, most of the really difficult work on the house had by now been completed.

It quite surprised me that on weekdays Vincent seemed content to stay at home all day with Andy without showing any interest in taking him out. He made sure that Andy had an afternoon sleep, sometimes cradling him in his arms while he slept until he woke up. He had the television on for most of the day except for Fridays when he cleaned up. Sometimes I would come home to find Vincent staring out of the front window making comments about the way people parked their cars. 'These idiots have parked facing the oncoming traffic. Look at how close this idiot has parked to the car in front. Always make sure you that you park at the end of the row so that we can get out without a problem.'

He also complained at length about the amount of litter on the front steps, which had blown over from the row of shops next to our house. 'Are you blind or don't you care about this mess?' he would say with a scolding tone, showing intense irritation if I failed to notice empty bottles or drifting newspaper as I came into the house. Usually I would let his comments pass thinking that he was in a bad mood for some reason, most probably from exhaustion and back pain. It crossed my mind that he was overreacting and becoming obsessive. He seemed to feel that I did not care enough about the house. Yet it also struck me as too petty to allow myself to be drawn into a heated argument. I expected that, once the work on the house had been finally completed, Vincent would return to his good-humoured self.

About three months later on one particular afternoon, I had an appointment at the doctor's to find out the result of a pregnancy test. We had been trying for six months, and after I missed a period, it seemed fairly certain to me. I had enjoyed my first pregnancy, and the birth was without major complication. I was looking forward to expecting our second baby and was keen for Andy to have a brother or sister quite close in age. I was already over thirty years old and conscious of our original plan to have a third child eventually. When the test result came back negative, I asked the doctor why I might have missed a period. He said there could be a number of reasons and asked if I was worried about anything. Although I was beginning to feel ill at ease about Vincent's increasingly obsessive thoughts, this did not seem to be on a significant scale, and I tended to associate his cantankerous manner with the rather insular life he was leading. I naturally thought that this would soon change once he started to go out to work again. Besides, Dr King at the group practice did not make me feel sufficiently at ease to discuss such matters with him. My slight concern about Vincent at this stage was neither sudden nor recent, as his preoccupied thoughts had developed very gradually over time. It certainly did not strike me as in any way relevant to the fact that I had missed a period. Dr King asked me to repeat the test in two weeks in case the first test had been too soon.

'I've also made an appointment to see Dr King,' announced Vincent. 'I've been feeling so irritable. Maybe he can prescribe some treatment.'

I felt quite relieved. I was glad that Vincent had admitted to feeling irritable, as he always gave the impression at home that I was the main cause of his irritation, although I was very careful never to do anything to deliberately annoy him. I thought of Vincent's irritability as more of a social than a medical problem. I was therefore surprised when Dr King prescribed tranquillizers. Vincent was not keen to take the tablets, and took one only when he had difficulty getting to sleep. He was also prescribed painkillers, which he took when his back was particularly painful. I was glad that he used his medication sparingly, as it seemed unhealthy to become dependent on such medication in the long term.

Vincent was a very private person. He had always held the romantic notion that it was he and I against the rest of the world, emphasising that nothing should ever come between us. For me to discuss his problem with anyone would have felt like a betrayal. He did not like me to talk to anyone about our home life, his background, or even the work he was doing on the house. I failed to understand the reasons for this, but respected his wishes as far as possible. There were times when I made an occasional joke about going out to work for a rest after the hard work of mixing plaster or mortar, buying building materials, and looking after the baby. Teaching in a London secondary school including running a department was not exactly restful! As the changes in Vincent were so gradual, I became used to locking away my growing anxieties, which, in retrospect, I realize were so deep rooted that I failed to admit them to myself. Apart from the sheer physical exhaustion, which I considered to be the main reason for his irritability, I sometimes thought of his increasingly prickly manner as being a sign of crotchety eccentricity rather than anything more sinister.

Vincent now talked increasingly about people's resentment towards him because of his talents in building work. He became obsessed that people in the neighbourhood were dead set on preventing him from completing the work on the house. This made no sense to me, and I saw no evidence of it. However Vincent was utterly convinced, and his conviction was unshakable. When he was rebuilding the chimney stack, he had to haul a new chimney pot thirty feet up on to the roof. He had placed the chimney pot in the garden ready for the haul. When the neighbour's garden sprinkler sprayed part of our garden, as often happened, the water soaked the chimney pot making it even heavier to lift. Vincent interpreted this as a deliberate act. Clearly a wet chimney pot would be significantly heavier than a dry one. However, I simply could not accept that there was any deliberate malice. When I refused to accept his views, Vincent felt that I was running to the defence of other people and therefore betraying him. I was beginning to feel confused by his impressions that made little sense. I also began to feel isolated as well as trapped by the sense of betrayal, as I was unable to disclose my feelings to anyone about this. I thought that if Vincent could get back to a normal life by going out to work, he would benefit from wider social interaction, and he would soon regain a healthy sense of proportion in his views.

About a month after my first visit to Dr King, I received the result of the second pregnancy test. This time it was positive. I felt delighted. The baby would be due on my birthday. Vincent, on the other hand, showed no emotion or excitement. In fact, he felt disgruntled that the result of the original pregnancy test had been negative; he felt that the doctor was just giving us something to worry about. I dismissed such an idea and wished that he could share my joy. I was to finish work at the end of the summer term. When my pupils found out that I was expecting a baby, they began rushing to open doors and carry my books for me. I attended all my antenatal appointments, which were held first at our doctors' group practice where I saw Dr Singh regularly. Later the appointments would be at the hospital where I was to give birth.

I also went to the hospital for the ultrasound scan, which was a routine procedure for all expectant mothers at a fairly early stage in their pregnancy. By measuring the baby's bones they could establish very accurately the age of the baby and work out the expected date of confinement. It gave me great satisfaction and reassurance to see the image of the baby inside me. When the staff asked me to return for a second scan only two weeks later, I did not feel worried. They assured me that everything was fine and that they simply wanted to be more precise about the date. Vincent, however, reacted very differently. 'Why do you have to keep going for these ultrasound scans if everything is progressing normally?' he asked with a tone of great suspicion. 'I reckon it's their way of seeing if we would be flustered by the possibility of a complication.' Again this struck me as an unfathomable reaction.

'What possible motivation could they have for seeing if we'd be worried?' I asked, but received no response.

After the second scan, the date of expected confinement was revised to mid November, two weeks after my birthday. The pregnancy developed well; I ate well and gained weight steadily. I did not reduce my daily activities at all. I continued to take Andy and the dogs to the park practically every day. Vincent no longer showed any interest at all in taking them out. The last occasions when we had taken them out together had resulted in him getting very annoyed at me for failing to walk on the 'correct' side of the path or for changing from walking on one side of the path to the other. This notion made no sense to me.

Vincent began to prepare himself for a new job. He bought two new pairs of jeans and a new denim jacket. He was very particular about the jacket and returned it to the shop simply because there was an 'extra' buttonhole in the flap of one of the pockets, which was designed for a pencil to fit through. In the shop it took him ages to decide on a different jacket, and he kept asking for my opinion. I was very patient with him, and in the end he decided to keep the original jacket. It seemed as if he was probably feeling tense about the idea of going out to work and concerned about making a good impression.

Vincent appeared to have lost any vitality and zest for life. It was a very gradual change, and I had grown accustomed to his constant complaints of 'aggravation' from others. He had developed a foul temper, and I thought it wise to avoid doing or saying anything that could be construed as provocation. In particular, he could not tolerate flippant remarks.

'Why do people always watch me so closely in shops?' he asked.

'Maybe it's because you look like an escaped convict,' I joked, taking care not to go too far in teasing him. The fact was that he looked altogether quite respectable these days. Why then should he feel so sensitive about his appearance? I could only surmise that, again, it was anxiety and stress at the prospect of returning to the world of work. As he found shopping so stressful, rather than deal directly with shop assistants, he delegated almost all the purchasing to me. As well as doing the weekly food shopping, I would follow Vincent's detailed requirements for choosing tools and all kinds of building materials.

Although I had seen evidence of Vincent's temper quite early on in our relationship, it had been apparent only on rare occasions. After the successful party we had thrown in the basement flat after our first year together, I had been unable to find my keys. Vincent was furious at me for leaving them lying around and was convinced that someone at the party had taken them. I had been quite upset at the intensity of his anger, especially as it turned out that it was Vincent who had, in fact, picked up my keys and lent them to Nigel when he had gone out to buy some more drinks. Nigel had forgotten to return the keys to me. What also struck me at the time was that Vincent did not apologize to me; it was as if he had been perfectly justified in making such unfounded accusations.

On another occasion, when Bullet was still a young puppy, we came home after a late night out to find that Bullet had eaten Vincent's leather bootlaces. Vincent had been drinking heavily that night and was so angry that he beat Bullet hard, making him quiver with pain and fright. I felt terribly upset to see the poor animal suffer such harsh punishment and even more upset to see this vicious streak in Vincent. When he threw his boot at Bullet, I stepped forward to take the blow, which left a large painful bruise on my shin. Again, Vincent showed no sign of remorse. How could he fly into such a rage over such a small transgression? Was it the effect of alcohol? I found this difficult to deal with. Vincent, until that stage, had been affectionate and romantic towards me, and there were no other signs of conflict between us. He often used to say that we should never allow anything to come between us and that we should always put one another first. Now a hurtling boot had come between us, and a temper that seemed to take very little to ignite. Sometimes I wondered if his temper had played any part in the break-up of his previous marriages, since he had mentioned violent arguments in relation to his break up with April.

When Vincent lost interest in going to the pub for a drink, I felt pleased. If the effect of alcohol played any part in stirring his temper, then it was a welcome development. This coincided with the time when Nigel had moved out of our house. However, with this came a lack of interest in mixing socially even at home. I had always made his friends from work welcome and still enjoyed the company of friends and colleagues. Before he had stopped work to look after Andy and to work on the house, Vincent had resolved never again to invite to the house anyone from work. This struck me as strange, as he had seemed to enjoy socializing during the period after we had first met. He was still very critical of my work colleagues. Knowing that to invite them home would invade his privacy, I also decided to respect his wishes. I was mindful of what Vincent had told me about the reason for the breakdown of his marriage to April. He had felt that she was influenced by her friends, who had come between them. I enjoyed my home life immensely, especially now that we had started a family of our own. I expected to stay in more, so it seemed a small sacrifice to put a social life on hold. I thought that Vincent could be all things to me: companion, lover, provider, and protector.

The work that Vincent did on the house was never motivated, on his part, by any desire to impress others. On the contrary, his main consideration was to create pleasant surroundings that were practical to live in. Although he enjoyed recognition of his talents, he disliked the idea of showing people round the house. It struck him as an unwelcome intrusion. Although I would have felt very proud to show friends the house as evidence of Vincent's considerable talents and skills, I again respected his views on the matter.

The transformation of the bathroom was even more spectacular than that of the kitchen. Vincent spent five months on this room. He wanted to produce the effect of a dungeon. There were three steps leading down from the mezzanine level landing into the bathroom, which already gave the room a sunken effect. The ceiling alone took three weeks to complete. Worked in plaster in the design of a gigantic spider's web, it was totally original. Vincent stripped the plaster from the walls, exposing the bare brickwork, which he pointed and then wiped with a rag following the uneven contours of the bricks. Then he varnished them to bring out their varying colour tones. Along the entire length of the external wall, Vincent inserted a double row of glass blocks set in white mortar. He built a white sill, perfect for indoor plants. In the corner he made a recess where he fitted a glass shelf that was graced with a reproduction antique of an Assyrian head. He finished the bottom half of the exposed brick wall with blue patterned tiles which were stepped at different levels to correspond to the height of the toilet, wash basin, bidet, and bath. The room was a masterpiece in interior design. It was spacious, luxurious, unique, and very practical. There was ample shelf space, additional cupboard space under the washbasin and bath, as well as a very large airing cupboard. A large mirror on the chimney breast opposite the glass blocks reflected lots of light, and an opening window above the bath ensured adequate ventilation. On the surface of that windowsill I etched a primitive outline of Bullet, visible only when standing in the bath.

Home improvement during the late 1970s and early 1980s was by no means as widespread a craze as it subsequently became one or two decades later when DIY stores sprung up in every town, and television programmes on home improvement abounded. Vincent had an aversion to the term *DIY*, as he rightly regarded himself as a master craftsman of the highest order. It was his passion, and he became obsessive over attention to detail. His work far exceeded my own wishes and expectations. I would have preferred to have his company in the evenings and be sure he was in a balanced state of mind rather than see him exhaust himself, striving to complete work late into the night or the early hours of the morning. On several occasions he even worked right through the night. If I tried to protest about his working hours, he would overrule me by explaining that it was the nature of the task that dictated the pace.

After recovering from the marathon of the work on the bathroom, Vincent next worked on the living rooms to create a spacious, open-plan area. He knocked down the two walls that had separated the original reception rooms from the hallway and stairs, leaving one section to create a small inner porch inside the front door and a diagonal section following the line of the stairs at the other end of the room. He glazed the internal door of the porch to allow natural light to pass through. The two fireplaces formed the most interesting features of the living area. After he stripped the chimney breasts of plaster to expose the brickwork, he varnished them so that they contrasted against the soft apricot colour of the walls. He cast a raised white sill in each fireplace about eighteen inches above the level of the floor. He marked out the ceiling with timber and plastered in sections with a swirl design. Sparsely furnished, it was a bright, airy living area, an ideal place for Andy to play with his toys and learn to ride his first little bicycle.

The work in the main bedroom was to follow. This room was to have a stunning fireplace, again raised above floor level and with a sill cast in white concrete as well as a fireplace in the form of an egg with a square-shaped opening. Vincent had again worked through the night to complete the chimney breast, which he had laboriously covered with small segments of sand and cement applied to resemble fish scales. He had removed the ceiling to reveal the shape of the London roof, which dipped in the centre where the valley ran from the front to the back of the house. He clad this with timber giving a spacious, almost ecclesiastical impression. The loft section above the second bedroom was one of the few places where I was trusted to do some painting. Nevertheless, in spite of my best efforts, Vincent grumbled at me for failing to keep the paint evenly spread. Even in spaces that were not open to view, everything had to be completed to the highest standards.

Conscious of faults in his own work, Vincent was anxious to go over certain jobs again once he had completed everything else. Would we ever have a life free from this unrelenting labour? At the final stage, there remained all the window frames to be painted and the rear garden to be sorted out. We were finally very close to this stage of completion. Clearly the strain of the work so far had taken its toll on Vincent both physically and mentally. Even though he claimed that the pace of the work was determined by the materials he was using—for example, plaster or sand and cement which had to be applied quickly—many times he put himself under unnecessary strain by his insistence on a top-quality professional finish and a punishing schedule. He seemed frustrated by the limits set by the number of hours in a day and by the limits of reasonable human endurance. On the occasions when I suggested that our relationship was suffering from the effects of his exhaustion, he would reply that this was the price to pay for getting the work done. In other words, it was a temporary inconvenience that I simply had to put up with. However, I found increasingly that, even after long periods of rest and a complete break from the work, his irritability and bitterness were still clearly in evidence. These days he showed me very little affection. He would cast accusations that I failed to appreciate his work and that I was not interested in seeing the house completed. When in a calmer mood, he would tell me that all his efforts were motivated by the single aim to provide a comfortable family home.

Another recurring dream I had during our marriage revealed Vincent living alone in a small, cluttered rented flat ironing his clothes. In this dream he appeared somehow to have been abandoned. The interior decoration was dismal, with old-fashioned wallpaper and dark furniture, which was in sharp contrast to the bright, spacious, terraced London house where we now lived. Such a strange dream. The emotion of this dream was one of pity and an overwhelming need to reconnect after being cast adrift for a long period of time.

Now I realized that maybe the recurring dreams signified just how far our relationship had strayed over the years. What was the point of living together in a sumptuous palace when we spent no quality time with each other and when all that Vincent felt towards me appeared to be resentment and lack of trust? How could we navigate our way back to that intimate place where our relationship had felt secure and we could enjoy the simple things in life? Surely, I convinced myself, when the work on the house was truly over and we had our lives back with a new baby to focus on, everything would be fine, and Vincent would be content with the next phase in life.

Chapter 5

Alienation

By the time I resigned from my teaching job at the start of the school summer break, Vincent was ready to start his new job. He had soon found work. With his extensive experience in carpentry, obtaining a new job was not a problem. During those first few weeks, the weather was lovely, and I looked forward to each new day. I was so happy to be able to devote my time to looking after Andy. After Vincent got up in the morning, Andy would climb into bed with me and then wave to Daddy through the front bedroom window as Vincent set off for work. Now that Andy was almost two, it was a good time to start potty training. Much of my time was spent mopping up little puddles around the house, so I allowed Andy the freedom to leave his trousers off while he was at home. However, whenever Vincent came home from work, he insisted on him being fully clothed.

I liked to take the dogs out for their walk after breakfast when I had lots of energy. In the afternoons I started to take Andy to the playgroup in the park, which was held outside in the summer. It concerned me that, up to now, he had not mixed with other children at all. While I had been working full time, it had been difficult to get to know other mothers with young children in the locality. I was now really looking forward to launching Andy into toddler society and possibly making new friends myself. I also hoped that this would speed up Andy's speech development, which was limited for his age. He enjoyed his visits to the playgroup but needed me to be at his side the whole time. He particularly liked going on the small slides and pushing the little trucks around. On one day I took our camera and had a great time taking photos of him everywhere. I loved watching him playing with other little children. On our first visits, he wanted to kiss them and touch their hair. It was such a new experience for him. Most of the other children already knew each other quite well and were not very welcoming to newcomers. But Andy was happy playing on his own alongside the others and enjoyed the company around him.

When it was a matter of getting used to adults, Andy was very shy. On one morning in the park we met the woman who lived across the road from us. Her name was Chris. She was with her dog and young son, Simon, who was a year older than Andy. It was lovely to walk together round the park getting to know each other. We chatted about the playgroup, dogs, potty training, and things of interest in the locality and seemed to have a lot in common. I made a casual arrangement to see her later at the playgroup, and after that, we bumped into each other quite often. I enjoyed her company, and Andy got on well with Simon. Eventually she invited us in for a cup of tea, an invitation that I gladly accepted. When she offered to look after Andy for me when I went for my antenatal appointments, I thanked her for her kindness and explained that Andy was not used to being left with people he did not know well. I longed for the time when Andy could have Simon and other children round at home to play with, but I was reluctant to invite anyone until Vincent felt settled in his new job.

I used to look forward to Vincent coming home after work each day. It was tiring looking after Andy, and the heat of the summer weather made my legs ache. However, Vincent seemed unable to offer any help. He often worked late and seemed unable to relax at the end of the day. He talked to me all the time about the things he was involved with at work, and strangely had no time for Andy, which saddened me. I assumed that he simply needed more time to settle in at work. From the start he had been anxious that he might not find it easy to get a job although there was always a reasonable selection of vacancies for carpenters in the newspapers. Understanding that he needed a lot of reassurance, I was very patient and gave him support and encouragement during this anxious period.

Having found his vocation in life as a carpenter, Vincent generally found his work stimulating and satisfying. In the past he had enjoyed variety and had felt that his skills had been acknowledged and appreciated by his workmates and managers. He preferred working in Central London, saying that he felt from experience that people there had a different attitude to work compared to people who lived in South London. I did not fully understand this, as it seemed to me that the convenience of working nearer to home would reduce travelling time and avoid parking problems. I encouraged him to take a job nearby, and it was with a small local building firm that he got this first job.

In the first week he had to replace a window in a woman's house. He told me how much he disliked the woman, who complained too much about the time it was taking to complete the work. After working as fast as he could in order to get away from the woman and the pressure he felt, he was then able to start a different piece of work on the company office. He told me how much he liked his boss and felt that he got on well with him. Yet he still had little time for Andy. I had hoped that after work he would spend time with him in the evenings in a similar way that I had done when I had been going out to work. However he was far too preoccupied with his new job. He was eating very little at work and asked me to pack less for his lunch, as he would only end up bringing food back home uneaten. When he told me he only wanted fruit and a drink, as he did not want bread, I tried to persuade him to take some boiled eggs or a piece of cheese as well. I suggested some frozen snacks as a change from my home-baked brown rolls. He accepted the offer of sausage rolls and pork pies, so I made sure there was a stock of them in the freezer. Even so, he always brought some food back home untouched.

By the end of his second week at work, Vincent became preoccupied with a plan. His boss had to install a new toilet downstairs. He drew me a plan to show the layout and asked me for my opinion on an idea he had to improve the access to the office.

'It looks sensible to me,' I replied.

'Do you think I should show the plan to my boss?' Vincent asked me.

'I don't know. It's difficult for me to advise you on this,' I replied.

'It's a way I can show that I have ideas to benefit the company and be of some value. Up to now, the boss hasn't commented on my work, and I want to know what he thinks,' he said, pressing me to agree with his idea.

The next day, a Friday, in the middle of the morning, Vincent came home unexpectedly. My first thought was that maybe he was injured. 'Are you all right?' I asked.

'I've been sacked,' he replied, the disappointment showing on his face and in his voice. We sat down to talk. He told me that he had sensed a gradual change of attitude from his boss since he had started working there. When he submitted the plan, his boss showed little interest, and this prompted Vincent to ask him what he thought of his work. His boss took the opportunity to tell him, 'Well, as a matter of fact, I think you're too slow, and I've been thinking of getting rid of you.'

'In that case I'll go right now,' Vincent had replied, annoyed. He arranged to pick up his salary at a later date and came straight home.

After putting so much effort into his work, this came as a terrible blow to him. In carpentry he had always taken great pride in the quality of his work. He derived no satisfaction from slapdash methods with swift results, which was apparently all his boss had been interested in.

Vincent spent a few hours on the telephone determined to find another job that very same day. By two o'clock he had arranged to go and see someone about a vacancy. He came back later to announce that he was due to start this new job after the weekend. What a relief! Without the prospect of a new job, it would have been a very depressing weekend. To take his mind off the negative experience of being sacked, he decided to spend most of the weekend burning old paint off the walls inside the front porch in preparation for decorating the front of the house. He wanted to get this work on the front completed before the start of the winter by doing one section at a time each weekend. The painted rendering extended from the front porch down each side of the steps, round the bay windows of the basement and ground floor, and down the steps to the front door of the basement. It was a considerable area and a time-consuming job.

When Monday came, Vincent set off for his new job in Central London while I continued with my daily routine. It was difficult to handle the dogs now that Bailey was coming into season. Although there were no visible signs yet, Bullet kept trying to mount her, but he only did this when we were out in the park in full view of every passer-by. He never tried to mate with her in the house. At first I tried to stop him by putting him on the lead, which he hated. This only succeeded in exhausting me as he pulled with all his muscular might on the lead. When in exasperation I released him again, he persisted with his frantic efforts and annoyed Bailey to the extent that she bit his ears. As a result, Bullet developed a painful lump in his right ear. After Bailey had bitten his ears when she had been a puppy Bullet had already had one lump removed from his left ear, and the surgery had been successful. The vet did not consider the second lump to be serious, but Vincent did not accept his advice and arranged for surgery again. As it took a long time for his stitched ear to heal, I took the dogs for their walks separately. After his ear eventually healed, he was unable to hold the ear erect for a while, so he had one floppy ear and one erect. Vincent was downright annoyed and held me responsible for what he considered to be a serious disfigurement that resulted from my inability to control the dogs. Of course, on the rare occasion when Vincent took the dogs for a walk himself, Bullet and Bailey were on their very best behaviour.

A few days after Vincent started his new job, he asked me to phone his previous workplace and arrange for him to collect his salary and documents. The woman I spoke to explained that they would not have the cash until pay day, so she offered to put a cheque in the post with his documents, to which I agreed. At first Vincent said this was okay. Then after a while he questioned me about the exact words I had used and began to get annoyed. 'My cards can easily get lost in the post. Don't you realize that this could lead to a delay in getting my tax code sorted out? It's not as if I'm in any hurry to get my money. You must have given the impression that the money is all I'm interested in,' he said in a reproachful tone.

'If you're so concerned, why don't you speak to them yourself? You know, since you started back to work we've ceased to function as a family any more,' I replied taking the opportunity to speak my mind for once.

'You've let me down and betrayed me,' he retorted angrily.

How could he consider such a thought? Upset and confused, I could feel tears welling up; I was unable to hold them back. The pregnancy was making me more tearful than usual. Yet I had good cause to feel upset. There was so much to look forward to. Why could Vincent not see this? He seemed incapable of enjoying life.

'I think I'll go abroad for a while and find a job somewhere overseas,' he said completely out of the blue, showing not the slightest consideration for me, Andy, or the new baby who was due in about two months. I felt devastated. He picked up the car keys and walked towards the door. 'I'm going for a drive.'

Left sitting there feeling numb, I puzzled over the prospect of Vincent leaving us to work abroad, realizing all too well that whatever psychological problem he was suffering from was bound to follow him. I instinctively knew that there was no escape for him. I also knew in my heart that this was an empty threat. There was no way that he could control his enigmatic, depressed feelings.

In his new job, Vincent worked as part of a team with other carpenters. The first piece of work consisted mainly of boxing in pipes in old people's flats. Conscious of being watched closely by the other workmen, he felt very ill at ease. He expressed a strange uncertainty about the how to set about his work. Although I was accustomed to being asked for my opinion about the work he did on our house, it was a different matter entirely to be asked for my opinion or guidance about his job at work. I could only encourage him to consult the other carpenters in the team in order to be certain that he was doing everything correctly and in accordance with the procedures. I failed to understand why he lacked confidence and needed to seek so much reassurance in this way. As I had great faith in his abilities, I felt it was simply a matter of time before he settled in and felt at ease.

At lunchtime when the men went to the pub, Vincent did not feel like joining them. During the tea breaks he sat on his own feeling like a social outcast.

'Why don't you take the initiative to make conversation with the other guys?' I asked.

'Whenever I crack a joke, they don't seem to appreciate my sense of humour,' he replied. He was like the new boy starting at a new school where everyone else had already formed friendship groups. I was not at all used to seeing this submissive side to him; he seemed lacking in confidence, lonely, uncertain, and highly sensitive. Apparently he respected his boss and looked up to him as a father figure. By all accounts his boss was very patient with Vincent.

Still not eating properly, he became increasingly particular about his packed lunch. He objected strongly to the use of ice cream containers for his lunch box. I instantly changed them. Then, without any explanation, he developed an aversion to any food or drink from the fridge or freezer that had condensation on the packaging. As tiresome as this was, I was careful to store his cans of drink in a cupboard and to leave frozen food out overnight to ensure that defrosting was complete and the packaging was dry by the morning.

I recalled that Vincent had previously commented on his tea or coffee at work tasting strange. Once when he said the same about his drinks at home, I simply joked that it was just a small trace of arsenic. This sort of black humour appealed to him, as his own sense of humour was very much on the dark side.

He now inspected everything very closely: the individual wrapper of a chocolate biscuit, the cellophane round the pork pie, and even the skin on the fruit. Drinks had to be canned, not bottled. He told me that he had stopped drinking tea at work because he suspected that someone was putting something in it. When I asked him for the reason for being so particular about his food, he refused to tell me but was all the more insistent. Next he was adamant that each item of food should be wrapped only in sealed packaging, and he flatly refused to eat anything that I had wrapped myself. My thoughts suddenly unspooled and then collided as the realisation struck me that he must actually suspect me, too, of contaminating his food and drink. This was unbelievable! Was he so stressed that he was completely losing his mind? He was clearly depressed. Was it possible that depression could trigger such paranoia? It made me wonder if he had previously experienced such distorted perceptions earlier in his life. Furthermore, could something like this have been the cause of arguments that contributed to the breakdown of his former marriage?

Vincent was losing weight, and the situation was getting serious. His new jeans were already too loose round his waist, and his features looked gaunt. Although he was not eating properly, he was working at full capacity and unable to relax at home. It became more and more obvious that something was seriously wrong with his mental health and that a rapid deterioration was setting in. He came home from work only to announce that he needed to go all the way back again because he had realized on the way home that he had done something wrong. He felt he had to put it right before morning. Reluctantly, realizing that he would have no peace of mind until he had sorted out the problem, I felt powerless to protest.

Afterwards he was still unable to relax, and he started to ask me again about aspects of his work. He thought that it was not simply a matter of producing a finished job, but that the methods used needed to comply with the way the other carpenters worked. He said he was not supposed to use certain tools at work. Puzzled by this notion, I said it was ridiculous and I asked him why. He was unable to explain. It was little more than an impression that he had. I suggested, 'If it is the case that you're not supposed to use certain tools, you need to ask your boss.'

'No one has told me directly, but there are indications . . . signals. I understand that I can't use a tape measure and have to use a rule instead.'

'That doesn't make any sense. Why?' I asked.

'I don't know why,' he replied. 'There's too much to learn. I'm willing to learn, and I'm interested, but it's all so much effort.'

It was clear to me that Vincent was on the verge of some kind of mental breakdown. It was no longer helpful to think that once he had settled in at work everything would be fine. He needed to rest. He needed time to sort out this terrible demented confusion in his mind. I wondered what was the actual reality of the situation at his place of work. Towards the end of his first week with the firm, his boss told him that he was concerned about the slow pace of his work. In the evening Vincent asked for my advice about the piece of work he was trying to finish. 'I've cut the holes in the wood for the pipes. To finish the job I need to know what the significance is of the position of the pipes. I know it's something to do with to the colours.'

'What colours?' I asked.

'Red, blue, and white,' he replied. 'It's something to do with hot and cold. It's some kind of formula.'

'There can't be any special meaning other than the standard association of hot and cold with red and blue,' I said, trying to figure out what he could possibly be referring to. Most insistent that there was indeed some kind of secret formula that he needed to learn, he was convinced that, once he had grasped the formula, which everyone else knew, he would be able to complete the job in the correct way. We had not reached very far in this discussion when he suddenly picked up his car keys and headed straight back to work.

I realized that I could not put any pressure on Vincent, but I needed to find a way to persuade him to stop work and seek medical help. Instinctively I knew that it would be incredibly difficult to suggest to him that he had a serious mental problem. He was incapable of realizing that the source of his troubles, far from originating from external forces, was rooted in his own mind.

First I suggested that he should take a couple of days off to rest, because he was driving himself too hard. Though he did not object to this idea, he felt that he was so close to completing the job at work that he felt compelled to finish it off. We agreed that the work on the house could wait, as he already had too much going on in his mind. Yet in spite of this agreement, he came home early on the Friday of the summer bank holiday weekend and went straight outside to patch up the rendering above the front door of the basement. He assured me that it was a quick job. Soon after he set to work, I heard him swearing to himself, because the fresh sand and cement kept falling off as he tried to apply it.

In the end, he spent several hours on what was to be a quick simple job. It was a busy time of day when people were heading home from work, going to the shops next to our house, or going out for the evening. A couple of his old acquaintances, who had not seen him for a long time, stopped to have a quick chat with him. Vincent grew more and more impatient and simply wished that people would leave him alone to complete the work without distraction. Finally he lost patience altogether and gave up on the job. He was in a terrible mood and once again reproached me for failing to show any interest or contribute any constructive ideas for the completion of the work on the house. Each time he wanted to have a heated discussion or argument it was inevitably late in the evening when all I wanted was to collapse in bed and catch up on sleep. Sometimes I did not sleep well due to the stress I was under worrying about Vincent. Moreover, I always felt worn out at the end of the day after looking after Andy, who usually went to bed quite late himself, especially if he had had a long sleep in the daytime.

On the August bank holiday we took Andy to the London Zoo to celebrate his second birthday. We desperately needed a day out to relieve the tension. I took a picnic, but Vincent ate hardly anything at all. He showed no interest in taking any photos, so I took some myself of Andy with Vincent. He seemed a bit more relaxed as long as I was careful to let him dictate the pace and order of activities. If at any time I opposed him, be it over deciding what to take with us, where to park the car, which side of the path to walk on, the tension would begin to mount.

The following week, he finally agreed to take time off work. He had had a long talk with one of the other carpenters who was very sympathetic, and who had told Vincent that he had once come close to a nervous breakdown himself. His boss was also very understanding and told Vincent that his wife had had 'trouble with her nerves' and had taken Valium for a long time. I felt pleased that they had some understanding of mental illness and showed him sympathy.

Now that he was home, I was anxious that he should seek psychiatric help as soon as possible. I knew that the very suggestion would be abhorrent to him and that he would view any pressure on my part as interference, which would most certainly prove to be counterproductive. It was terrible having to wait, but I simply had no option. I had to leave him to come to this conclusion of his own accord. After a day or two, I asked Vincent if he would get a certificate from the doctor so that he could claim sickness benefit.

'There's nothing wrong with me, so I feel it's dishonest to claim sickness benefit.'

'It's by no means dishonest. You're absolutely exhausted. If you don't take time to rest, you'll only feel worse.'

Finally he agreed to think this over.

Meanwhile, as the school term started, I began to take Andy to the playgroup at a nearby school. We went there every Tuesday and Thursday afternoon. Andy enjoyed this but still needed me to be at his side most of the time. I looked forward to the opportunity to chat with the other mothers. I saw Chris and Simon from across the road there regularly and soon made friends with other mothers who attended regularly. To help Andy to settle into a routine of mixing with the children, I also decided to attend the Wednesday afternoon craft classes for mothers with toddlers. I enjoyed getting on with some sewing while Andy played. As the weather stayed fine, Vincent decided to continue with his work on the front of the house. Having burnt the paint off the basement window, he prepared to start painting when suddenly he called me downstairs into the basement to ask my advice. 'Should I start painting from the left or the right? I don't want to do it wrong.'

I thought how strange that he should ask such a thing. I put my arms round him and struggled to hold back my tears. 'It doesn't matter where you start. There is no wrong or right about it. Just choose a place to start without thinking about it.'

Oblivious to the fact that I was embracing him, he simply stood there looking confused with his arms hanging limply by his sides. He seemed so helpless. He urged me to decide for him, unable to accept that there was no question of right or wrong. In the end I advised him to start in the top left-hand corner. When he was half way through painting the window he called me downstairs again. This time he started talking about the money we had in savings. We had always kept our savings, which amounted to about three thousand pounds, in my bank account. The mortgage payments were debited from this account. Vincent liked to keep only just enough in his account to cover the standing order for his life insurance payments. Almost all our spare money had been spent on materials and fittings for the house. 'I want you to go and draw out half our savings from your account in cash,' he said, 'so that it can be paid into mine.'

I was getting tired of his suspicions about me. To eliminate his mistrust, I agreed to transfer the money without delay. As I was getting ready to do this, he called to me again saying not to bother. I told him that I insisted and set off for the bank, taking Andy with me. Having drawn out the cash from my bank, I then drove to his bank to pay it in. Just as I was waiting in the queue Vincent appeared.

'Pay it straight back into your account,' he said. 'I have a minicab waiting, so I have to go.'

He disappeared as suddenly as he had appeared, eager to continue his painting. I stood there astounded and only after he had gone did it occur to me that we could have gone home together in our car.

Vincent talked more and more about the idea of going abroad, which left me feeling puzzled and concerned. It was unclear at first whether he intended to take a holiday or look for work. He complained about the UK and the fact that people here failed to appreciate his work. He somehow had the impression that people were more interested in being part of a social group. He felt alienated from such groups and annoyed by their practices, which he was certain excluded him. He even complained about the English language, taking offence at words that have a double meaning. Our savings did not amount to much, and the prospect of Vincent holding down a job was beginning to look uncertain. I was therefore reluctant to agree to money being spent on a holiday. On the other hand, I thought that it could be worthwhile if Vincent came back feeling rested and recovered. As for the idea of him going abroad to work, this struck me as entirely inappropriate. With my experience of working in Switzerland, Germany, and Sweden I knew how isolating and disorienting it could be, even though I spoke the languages there. 'I honestly think you would be very unhappy in a country where you don't speak the language,' I said. 'Apart from the fact that life would be very lonely and difficult, I don't understand how you could consider leaving us. The baby is due soon. Andy is only just two years old.'

'So what would you think of me if I left to work abroad like my father did?' he asked. 'After all the work I've done on the house, I think I have every right to go.'

'You've worked incredibly hard to create a beautiful home for us,' I conceded. 'Because of this, I could never feel justified in criticising or condemning you for leaving. I just don't understand your reasons for wanting to leave.'

Maybe I had underestimated the effect on Vincent that his father had had on him. The fact that his father had played no part in his early childhood—the most formative years—would obviously make him feel neglected. Then, to be reunited with his father only to find him harsh and controlling would be a bitter blow. The hostility of the family was bad enough, but then for them to abandon him as they dispersed around the globe would be like the final twist of the dagger. Without a role model, maybe Vincent simply failed to fully understand his own role as a father. However, I was trying to apply a logical explanation to a situation that clearly operated on a level that was far from rational.

What I felt unable to tell Vincent was that I thought he was terribly disturbed and that going abroad would most probably worsen his state of mind. I realized that he lacked the insight to see that it was his own deluded self that was the problem rather than anyone else's doing. His perception was extremely distorted. Clearly he was simply trying to make some sense out this jungle of confusion. In his mind, this involved heaping all blame and responsibility on external factors and other people. And it appeared that this included me as a main instigator.

One evening I asked him outright if he felt that I was in any way responsible for his depression. He dismissed the notion outright, which made me feel relieved. He was convinced that it was his workmates and his boss who were responsible for his state of mind. Now that he was no longer at work, it seemed that his impressions of the people at work, including his boss, had changed for the worse. As well as resenting his talents and abilities, he now felt that they had been mocking him. He swore that never again would he work in this country as a carpenter.

To make matters worse, Vincent began to experience real difficulty sleeping. He would get up in the early hours and go downstairs. He was smoking heavily. Then he started to go out in the middle of the night for a drive. One night in particular he went for a very long drive, and when I drove the car the next day I noticed that the engine was heating up very quickly, so I checked the water and oil. I wondered how Vincent could possibly have driven so far without realizing just how low the oil level was. He was normally most particular about keeping the car well maintained.

During another restless night, he got up and drank pint after pint of water as if to flush out his system. The next day he refused to drink any tap water at all and also refused to let Andy drink any. For a while he insisted that the dogs drink only cooled boiled water. Obviously he believed that our water supply had somehow been contaminated. He felt that he was being drugged. I continued to drink tap water to prove him wrong.

It was also during this period of restless nights that Vincent got distracted when working on the front of the house. He had aimed to finish the work so that it was sealed against the winter weather. Although he managed to finish painting the front windows, he was very sensitive to the remarks made by people passing by. He was convinced that they were referring to him all the time. Moreover, he interpreted their comments as criticism of the work he was doing. A mere gesture became an indication that he had done something wrong. If he heard laughter, he believed it was aimed at him and he would mutter words of abuse in response. It annoyed him intensely that people used such indirect methods to tell him things. It was yet another classic case of paranoid reactions.

Before he had finished repairing a crack in the windowsill, he started to fiddle with the head of an old pipe that was protruding from the wall opposite the window. The pipe had a vent fitted at the end to cap it. Having removed the vent, he then cleaned it till it was spotless, painted it white, and then put it back on the pipe. He asked me if he should remove one of the ears on the bracket of the pipe where it was to be refitted on the wall. At first I failed to understand what he meant. I had not been watching what he was doing and could not understand why he was spending so much time on this. When he saw my puzzled expression, he grabbed me roughly by the nape of my neck and pushed me to show me where the pipe was. This set me in a panic. Why was the pipe so important to him when he was supposed to be finishing the sill? Why should he be so annoyed at me and want to humiliate me in this way? He treated me like a foolish child in much the same way as I had seen him treat Nigel in the past.

A trail of unfinished jobs was to follow. He agonised over decisions, puzzled over what he had done wrong, spent long hours on the most insignificant tasks, and talked about the fact that he was not supposed to be using a lead light when his work extended into the dark evenings, saying that this was against the rules. When he showed me the airbricks he had fitted, I noticed that he had meticulously filled the holes in the top left-hand corner and the bottom right-hand corner with mortar. When I asked him why he had done this, he avoided answering. No doubt this was one of his strange associations.

It disturbed me to think that he was wasting time and energy on useless preoccupations. It alarmed me to think how misguided he was. I wondered if he felt compelled to do these things in an effort to create some order in his confused mind. Encouragement or discouragement on my part were to no avail. I decided to leave him to his preoccupations, as it appeared that he was not doing any harm and was not under any external stress, only that which was self-imposed.

In fact, things were steadily growing worse. Finally it proved just too much for him to finish the work outside on the front of the house. He spent a few days on strange preoccupations inside the house. This included the best part of an afternoon rearranging the things that I kept on the kitchen windowsill: a set of orange weighing scales, a blue-and-white dish containing tomatoes and plums, and a basket of apples and pears. He seemed to find a wealth of significance in the colours, especially red, blue, and white, and he strove to organize the items in a correct order. The height of each object as well as the association between the colours became significant to him in relation to left and right, up and down. Furthermore he believed that the neighbours who lived opposite, whose kitchen window faced ours, would be able to interpret the formula that these objects represented. He felt that the arrangement was some kind of signal to them.

When he enlisted my help in arranging the items, I did not wish to get involved. I had better things to do with my time. But I had to be patient with him.

'It's important that I get it right,' he said calmly.

'Look, there's no question of such things being wrong or right. Neither can they be of any significance to anyone else,' I explained as I did not want to encourage his deluded ideas. But I stayed with him for a while, as I did not want to appear to be too dismissive or impatient. At the end of the afternoon, he instructed me very firmly not to place anything on the windowsill. If I left even a bag of flour there while I was cooking, he would get very annoyed with me.

To help him to relax, Vincent started to drink alcoholic drinks in moderation. Since he had stopped going to the pub, we normally drank very little; in fact, we still had bottles of drink left over from the previous Christmas, nine months ago. He seemed better tempered after a drink, and it did help him to relax, at least for a period of a few days. This was followed by a very changeable period when he started going without sleep completely. One morning he got in the car only to get out and come straight back into the house. 'So I'm not supposed to drive the car now, am I?' he said.

'What do you mean?' I asked.

'Oh nothing,' he replied unwilling to give any explanation. Later that day, when I got in the car and had difficulty getting it into first gear, I wondered if he had interpreted this as a sign that he should no longer drive. He would call a mini-cab at around nine in the evening and come home in the early hours without saying where he had been or whom he had been with. I worried about him going out in this confused state of mind and always felt relieved when he came home. On one occasion he was out all night, and he did not come home till nine o'clock the next morning. Again he refused to tell me where he had been. After about a week of this, I was also concerned about the amount of money he was spending. Then to my relief he also expressed concern about his spending and finally announced that he was going to stay at home and rest. When I later asked him again what he had been doing night after night he said he had just been walking the streets. I found this hard to believe.

At this point in time, Vincent seemed to be extremely low in spirits. When he said that life was no longer worth living and started to talk about committing suicide, I felt really alarmed. Somehow I had to persuade him to seek psychiatric help. I still feared that any attempt to do this could cause more harm than good. I began by urging him to find someone he felt he could talk to and trust. By this time I realized that there was a limit to how much help I could give him myself. It simply was not enough to be patient, loving, and reassuring. It would take a third party to help him understand that the problem lay in his own head. But who?

Vincent looked through his address book. First he phoned an old friend he had not seen for a year or two, but he did not get far in the conversation before he realized that this was not the right person to talk to. Next he tried to trace one of his old colleagues from a couple of years ago. No luck! The firm had gone into liquidation.

Finally Vincent turned to me and said, 'I think you'd better find me a psychiatrist. I can't take any more of this.'

The sense of relief overwhelmed me. Without showing my immense relief in case it unnerved him, I simply replied, 'Okay.'

As I cast my mind back in an effort to pinpoint the landmarks that triggered the changes in Vincent's state of mind, I realized that the stress of working on the house was one trigger, though this stress was largely self-imposed. The prospect of becoming a father had seemed like a heavy responsibility, and there had been some signs of stress when I had been in hospital having our first baby, but these stress points appeared to be short-lived. The social isolation of his role as a stay-at-home father seemed to be a contributory factor, though this role had not actively prevented him from going out more. Above all else, it seemed that his return to work after an interval of eighteen months had been the major turning point.

I even wondered if Vincent's previous changes of career might have been in some way prompted by bouts of mental illness in the past. He had never referred to his own mental health before. When we had first met he would sometimes refer to people with mental health problems as 'nutters'. Yet the sudden drastic change from working as a musician when on the brink of commercial success, then working as a model, and finally finding peace of mind as a carpenter suggested that maybe stress had been a significant factor in his professional life. If this was the case, it also suggested that, with time, Vincent was capable of recovering his sanity and moving on successfully.

I often wondered to what extent my own responses and reactions might have contributed to his condition. Should I have been more dismissive of his delusions, or should I have been more accepting? Should I have challenged him more even at the risk of provoking aggression? Should I have betrayed his insistence on privacy and gone in search of guidance? When I catered to his whims rather than standing up to him, it was at least partly out of concern that our young son should not witness any outright conflict or acts of aggression. As I was pregnant again, I was also concerned about any potential risk of physical harm from his unleashed temper. So I played it safe.

More than anything, I longed for guidance on how best I should deal with Vincent's odd behaviour. I felt incredibly isolated and confused. I still loved Vincent. I could not reveal to my parents or sister how I felt. They had already formed their opinions of him long before there had been any visible sign of his instability. I had made attempts to make new friends at the playgroup, but I could hardly open my heart to them and reveal the intimate details of our home life. How was I to describe to anyone what was happening? My betrayal of Vincent's confidence in me would cause untold damage to our relationship. Now that Vincent had finally asked to see a psychiatrist, I would have the opportunity to express my anxieties and get professional advice. Giving information about him to medical professionals was clearly for his own benefit, so the notion of betrayal seemed invalid. I was relieved that this breakthrough had come well before the expected date of the new baby. There were six weeks left.

Chapter 6

Appointments and Disappointments

First I looked through the Yellow Pages of the telephone directory, but there were no psychiatrists listed separately. Doctors and surgeons were all together in one long section. Then I remembered the psychiatric hospital just a couple of miles away, which was where pupils with mental heath problems were referred from the school where I had worked. Vincent was not downstairs when I rang up to enquire. Straight away the charge nurse asked me the nature of the problem. I was able to speak frankly about my concerns that Vincent was disturbed, was feeling that he was being watched, and was unable to concentrate. Once she understood that Vincent had suicidal feelings, she urged that he should attend the emergency clinic without delay. Normally the hospital preferred patients to be referred by their family doctor, but I explained that Vincent was set against the idea of seeing him and that I had been unable to persuade him.

I wondered if I was doing the right thing to choose a hospital close to home in case Vincent became suspicious in the same way that he felt about working in the local area. I also wondered if it might be better for him to make the enquiries himself in case he became suspicious of me. As he was quickly losing patience and seemed to be on the brink of serious depression, there was no time to lose. I explained to him about the emergency clinic, and we set off straight away taking Andy with us.

First Vincent had to see a registrar who noted a lot of details about him and his background. Then we sat and waited for a consultation with a doctor. Vincent was very distant towards me. Andy had fallen asleep on the way there and, whereas Vincent would normally have carried him, he had left me to struggle to carry him from the car into the clinic and to a waiting room. He disliked the idea of registering at the hospital as he felt as if this was the beginning of a process of being certified insane. We had a very long wait of several hours. I was feeling tearful because of Vincent's hostility towards me, which became more and more tangible, but I battled to hold back the tears. After about three hours I took Andy home, leaving Vincent on his own for his appointment. About half an hour after I left, he was finally interviewed by a doctor. They asked him to return the following day for a further interview.

Vincent was very vague about the nature of the interview and was clearly unwilling to talk about it. All he told me was that the doctor had said the problem was very common, and he described Vincent as a very sensitive man. This was interpreted by Vincent as evidence that there was nothing clinically wrong with him.

The next day we all set off again for the emergency clinic. This time I had worked out a quicker way to get to the waiting room, which for some odd reason aroused Vincent's suspicion, and again he grew hostile towards me. It was the same procedure as the day before of waiting for several hours to be seen. Vincent expressed his annoyance to the nurses on duty at the reception desk. I had to admit that, for patients with mental health problems, the long wait was very discouraging. Fortunately Andy had fallen asleep in my arms. Vincent grew more and more impatient as time passed and kept asking the desk clerk how many patients were before him in the queue. Finally he set himself a deadline of three hours. When the three hours elapsed and he had not been called to be seen, Vincent gave the staff a piece of his mind about the hospital and announced that he would see a doctor privately elsewhere.

I wondered how many others like Vincent desperately in need of help would walk away exasperated by the long wait. After all, these are not people who can sit calmly reading a magazine or making polite conversation. It was bad enough for me having to wait for hours in that stuffy, smoky atmosphere. While I sympathised with Vincent, I felt bitterly disappointed at the failed attempt after help had been so close at hand.

Vincent was angry with me for what he saw as a deliberate attempt to get him certified. 'Look, Nicki,' he said. 'I know what you're up to. You just want to get me certified so that they'll lock me up in the loony bin. Do you think I don't know that you want to have the house to yourself?' He was afraid that, once details of his condition were on his medical records, they could be used as evidence against him in the future. I flatly denied such motives and tried to reassure him. We talked briefly about the possibility of a private consultation. Although it was worth considering, especially if this inspired Vincent with greater confidence and trust, it struck me that it would be beyond our financial means, as he would clearly need more than just a couple of consultations to remedy his problems.

At Vincent's request, I began to make telephone enquiries. It was explained to me that even seeing a psychiatrist privately would require a referral by the family doctor, and there was no way round this system. All along Vincent had shown great reluctance to see Dr King. He did not regard himself as being ill, had no wish to be certified as sick, and persisted with his refusal to claim sickness benefit even after several weeks off work. When I explained the referral system to him, he finally agreed to see the family doctor. That morning he came home with a certificate specifying depression, which he posted off to work. He also had an appointment at the outpatients' department of the same hospital where he had attended the emergency clinic. Vincent told the doctor that he had been manipulated by his work colleagues and also told him about his insomnia and restlessness. The hospital appointment was for the same day, which was a Tuesday, and the doctor had asked him to go without delay. Nevertheless he showed every intention of taking his time.

I had been under the impression that the GP he had seen was Dr King until he told me it was in fact Dr Singh. I had always found Dr King to be aloof and abrupt, though in the past Vincent had got on well with him, feeling he could talk to him man to man. He liked the way that he brought things down to a common-sense level. On the other hand, I much preferred Dr Singh, whom I saw regularly as my antenatal doctor when I was expecting Andy and whom I saw now every two weeks during my second pregnancy. He was always very pleasant, took an interest in my job when I was teaching, and called me by my first name, whereas Dr King never even remembered my name. Dr Singh was also very kind to Andy when I took him with me. So when Vincent revealed that it was Dr Singh he had seen, I was pleased. I had my next antenatal appointment with him on that same day, Tuesday, in the afternoon. Without discussing this with

Vincent, I had decided to tell the doctor just how worried I was, hoping that he could give me some advice. I felt unable to mention any of this to Vincent. I was afraid that to do so would provoke him, as he was in such a volatile state.

That Tuesday afternoon as I got ready to go to my appointment, Vincent told me to sit down in a most menacing tone. He began shouting at me in very strong abusive language. 'Before you met me you lived in filth. Now look at you, trotting around as if you are a queen, you sly creep. You're a snake.'

I felt completely taken aback. After this tirade of insults, I felt indignant and hurt that he could say such things to me. This was totally uncalled for and entirely unprovoked. I could only imagine that he thought that I intended to collude against him by discussing details of our home life with the doctor. Now I could hardly wait to tell the doctor just how serious the situation had become. My conscience was clear. How was I supposed to help Vincent if I had to keep information all to myself? I could not allow his paranoia to paralyse me.

The dogs were visibly upset by the hostile atmosphere and started scuttling about looking for an escape. I took Andy's hand and made for the door sensing that Vincent might not let me go after what he had just said. He got up and tried to stop me, but I struggled and protested. Andy moved out of our way, but the dogs pushed towards the door at the same time as I was trying to get through it.

'Let me go!' I screamed, but Vincent refused. As he pulled me back from the door, I scratched my hand on the catch, and both dogs made a run for it. As our house was on a busy main road, they were never allowed out without a lead.

'Now look what you've done!' scolded Vincent. I dashed outside to get hold of the dogs, who were trembling and panic stricken like me, but it was difficult as neither of them had a collar on. Whenever Vincent showed aggression at home, the dogs would tremble and pull their ears back. As I was in an advanced stage of pregnancy, I was unable to pick them up. I was calling at them to come to me, but they were agitated and confused. Andy was watching through the front window, and behind him stood Vincent watching as well. I felt so angry with him standing there, as if to say that I had brought this all on myself and so it was up to me to sort it out. There were several spectators standing outside the shop next door, but nobody was prepared to step forward to help. I sat down on the front steps to catch my breath, and I realized that people were afraid that the dogs might bite. I called out to a couple of youths reassuring them that the dogs were harmless, and it was with their help that I managed to get them both back into the house.

Leaving Andy at home, I walked across the road and, as soon as I was out of view, ran as fast as I could to the doctor's. Shaking and in tears, I went straight to the receptionist's room and asked if I could wait there instead of the waiting room. I calmed myself down. Dr Singh came in, and I asked if I could see him urgently. It was time for my appointment anyway. I began to explain what had just happened, and the doctor asked me if we had had a row. Telling him about the abusive language and aggressive behaviour, I felt the tears welling up again. I explained how deeply disturbed Vincent was and gave a few examples.

'You mean he's paranoid?' said Dr Singh.

'Yes, extremely paranoid,' I confirmed, relieved to be able to be brief. I then explained about Vincent's insomnia, his nocturnal wanderings, and some of the reasons it had taken me so long to come and confide in him. I added the fact that all Vincent had wanted out of life was a family, a home and a steady job, that now that these dreams were so close to being realized it was all falling apart. I explained about the off-putting wait at the psychiatric hospital and the fact that he still had not attended for his appointment that same morning.

The doctor was very sympathetic and rang the hospital to arrange for Vincent to be seen straight away.

'You love him very deeply,' he said recognising my devotion, at which it was impossible to hold back the sobs. He reassured me and gave me time to calm down. I felt so grateful to him.

'Are you worried about going home?' he asked, as if reading my mind.

'Yes, a bit.'

But I felt that I had no option. I needed to make sure Vincent went to the hospital without delay. I needed to check that Andy was okay.

When I got home, Andy was asleep on the sofa, and the dogs had calmed down. I told Vincent that, if he left for the hospital immediately, he would be seen straight away. I did not say any more than that, and Vincent left immediately. He returned later with a prescription for sleeping tablets and an appointment card. He told me he had a follow-up appointment the next week. I felt disappointed at the prospect of waiting another week. I had expected there to be some sense of urgency about his condition. To prescribe sleeping tablets to a potential suicidal victim struck me as highly questionable. Vincent was opposed to the idea of taking sleeping tablets, but he fetched them from the chemist's anyway. When I looked at Vincent's appointment card, I saw that there was no appointment written on it. This struck me as odd, so I rang the hospital to ask the reason. I was told that the system involved seeing whichever doctor was available at each visit, implying a long wait each time and quite possibly a different doctor. It struck me as a ridiculous system, as if designed from the outset to put patients off who had already all the odds stacked against them. I decided to talk to Dr Singh about this the following day.

When I talked about this to Vincent, he said he would prefer to go to a different hospital. Although Dr Singh was willing to make an appointment at a different hospital, his recommendation was to stay with the original one because he had confidence in the staff there. I felt anxious to give my account of what had happened. I was growing increasingly concerned about Vincent's paranoia and the real prospect that Vincent's hostility could centre on me with violent consequences. I was beginning to feel afraid of him. Before I had confided in the doctor, Vincent had probably guessed that this was my obvious intention. I was therefore losing his trust. It would have been too dangerous for me to talk about Vincent to doctors with him present. I asked Dr Singh to arrange for Vincent and me to be interviewed at the hospital separately, and he made the necessary arrangements as requested.

Before we left for our appointment, Vincent asked me if we should first get rid of a pile of rubble which had accumulated from the work he had done. He wanted to get it out of the way and, although I was anxious to get to the hospital as soon as possible, I did not wish to put him under pressure by showing my impatience. We therefore loaded the bags of rubble into the car and drove round to the local depot. Vincent was angry that I did not help him to unload the heavy bags. He was in a terrible mood and nagged at me claiming that I never lifted a finger to help. I resented this as, not only was it untrue, but I was heavily pregnant. This would be obvious to anyone else. I failed to understand how he could be so incredibly hostile.

He made no allowances for my condition, never asked how I felt, and showed no interest in the baby's development. He seemed totally self-absorbed. As for his involvement with Andy's upbringing, he now showed a very intolerant attitude. Potty training was still a hit-and-miss affair. Whereas I found it more practical to let Andy run round at home with no trousers or underpants on, Vincent would get even more annoyed with him if he did not put his clothes back on straight away. On one particular evening Vincent called to Andy in a commanding tone of voice, 'Come here.' Andy knew that Vincent was annoyed and stayed by my side looking afraid. Vincent repeated in an even more threatening tone, 'I said, "Come here!"' A tremendous sense of dread came over me. I could not look at Andy, who was still beside me. Suddenly Vincent seized him and smacked him really hard on his bare bottom making him quiver and scream. 'That'll teach you to run about with no trousers on!' he said. 'Don't take any notice of Mummy. She's a waste of time.'

Tears welled up in my eyes. Andy was screaming with pain. It had been a really hard smack. I could not bear to look at Andy or Vincent.

'You don't like that, do you?' he said to me. I shook my head, unable to believe that this was the man I had chosen to be the father of my children. I felt ashamed of myself for allowing such a thing to happen to my child. I wanted to comfort Andy, who was lying on the sofa sobbing but I could not move. Feelings of hatred for Vincent now began to make me feel highly conflicted.

I wondered how deeply Andy was being affected by the atmosphere and tension. He had often had miserable tantrums when he would cling to me and moan, usually because he felt tired or frustrated. Vincent claimed that he never behaved like this when I was not there. He would not tolerate moods or tantrums and would send him straight upstairs, refusing to allow him back down until he had stopped crying. On this occasion when Vincent had smacked him, Andy had previously been in a good mood. The smack was totally unjustified. If Vincent wanted to get at me, how grossly unfair it was to use Andy as the means. I did not dare speak my mind, as this could have provoked more aggression, but my body language said it all.

When we arrived at the psychiatry department, we had to wait for a while, then Vincent was called in for his interview. Andy was being difficult, running around and wearing me out. It was hot in the building, and I was sweating. Eventually Vincent came out, and I was called. The psychiatrist asked me what kind of man Vincent was. After I told him that he was serious and hard working, the interview developed and I explained my anxieties about his paranoia. The doctor suggested he should spend some time in hospital, if only to give me a break. I knew Vincent would not agree to a stay in hospital and thought that the whole idea was to help him directly, rather than simply give me a break. The doctor said he would prescribe some tablets.

'How do the tablets work?' I asked.

'They'll make the paranoia fade away,' replied the doctor.

'But how can drugs wipe out damage caused by external factors?' I asked, assuming that Vincent's condition was at least in part the result of environmental pressures. The doctor shrugged his shoulders and seemed uninterested in helping me to understand, as if to say, 'Take it or leave it. It makes no difference to me. It's your problem.' I desperately needed information about this kind of mental illness. I strongly suspected that Vincent would refuse to take the medication. I felt a mixture of anger, confusion, and despair.

The doctor said he would make another appointment for a week's time. I asked for some reassurance that Vincent would be seen by the same doctor at the next appointment.

'I'm sorry,' he replied. 'This is my last day here today. I'm leaving. But don't worry. I'll pass your notes on.'

This was the last straw. Just how many doctors and appointments would it take before we could get some real help? Appointment indeed! More like disappointment of the highest order!

Chapter 7

Delusions

As I had anticipated, Vincent refused both hospitalisation and medication. During my interview with the doctor, Andy had fallen asleep in Vincent's arms. I gently tried to help Vincent put Andy's jacket on, but he was in such a hurry to leave the hospital that he tugged the jacket aggressively and ripped it as he hurried to fit his arms into it. On our way home in the car I could see that Vincent was still very angry with me. 'Just wait till we get home,' he said in his threatening tone, his eyes glaring. 'I'm going to strangle you.'

I parked the car in front of the house and sat there wondering what to do. I felt so pathetic. On the one hand I felt genuinely frightened, taking his threat seriously. On the other hand, it seemed ridiculous to run up to someone and say, 'Help me! My husband has threatened to strangle me.' I told Vincent that I felt afraid, hoping that he would tell me he had not meant his threat to be taken literally. We went into the house, and Vincent went straight to the bathroom. He took a box of tampons out of the cupboard and went through them one by one.

'What's wrong?' I asked.

'I know you have something implanted inside you,' he said 'You agreed to have it done, didn't you!'

I could scarcely believe this. It was such a gruesome notion that it made me shudder. Had he gone completely out of his mind? Could he actually believe that I had had some kind of device implanted and that I had given consent for some kind of weird treatment?

'Do you think I don't know that your ultrasound treatment is affecting me?' he added.

'That's a positively grotesque idea,' I told him, which simply angered him all the more. I left him breaking up each of my tampons and felt like rushing straight to Dr Singh, but it was outside surgery hours.

That night in bed I could hardly sleep. I had put a plastic cover over the mattress under the sheet in case I went into labour and my waters should break. This made the bed feel hot. When Vincent turned over and touched my body he suddenly drew his hand away. 'I just felt an electric shock when I touched you,' he said, startled.

'Don't be ridiculous,' I responded shuddering at the thought of him being so deluded. Vincent went to sleep downstairs taking Andy down with him. He was obviously convinced that the 'device' was affecting our son as well. As I tossed and turned in bed, I decided to visit Dr Singh the following morning after my antenatal appointment at the hospital.

My antenatal appointments now alternated between the Dr Singh and the hospital. In the later stages of pregnancy, the hospital usually took over from the family doctor, but I needed to continue to see Dr Singh. Leaving Andy with Vincent, I set off for my hospital appointment. As I sat in the waiting room, tears started to well up. I was thinking of the events of the previous day. When I was called for my check-up, a doctor I had not seen before attended to me. His name was Dr Wardle. I had not gained any weight for the last few weeks, which was hardly surprising. I told the sister on duty that I had problems at home and that I had confided in my family doctor. Dr Wardle felt my tummy and looked at my card. The sister told him that I had problems at home.

'The baby feels a bit small for your dates, Mrs Adams,' said Dr Wardle. 'I think we'll have another scan done.'

His mouth dropped open as he watched my reaction. My face creased up and my body heaved convulsing with sobs that I had been trying to hold back all morning. 'My husband is completely paranoid,' I sobbed. 'He has this weird idea that I'm receiving special treatment with the scans and he thinks he's being affected by the ultrasound waves.'

They sat me up and reassured me that I did not have to have another scan if I did not want one. As I began to tell them a bit more about what was going on at home, it occurred to me that I really ought to be talking to Dr Singh. They agreed that I should see him straight away and arranged to see me again the following week, reassuring me that there would be no change of staff for my next appointment. They were very kind.

I drove straight to the doctor's surgery and told Dr Singh about Vincent's latest delusions. 'He really ought to be in hospital,' said the doctor.

'What kind of treatment would he be given?' I asked.

'He'll have the best of everything. Don't worry at all, Nicki,' he replied. But that did not reassure me.

'Do you think he would be given shock treatment, for example?' I asked, remembering my aunt who had to have treatment for her mental health problems.

'No, not shock treatment,' he replied, then admitted, 'I don't know much about the treatment of paranoid schizophrenia.'

This was the first time the term *schizophrenia* had been mentioned. The term startled me, as it had not occurred to me that this could be the name of the illness that had taken possession of Vincent. I did not really have much of a clue about what the nature of schizophrenia was, other than the commonly accepted notion that it was something like a split personality. I recalled a film I had seen in the 1960s called *Family Life*, and the humane approach to schizophrenia by the psychiatrist R.D. Laing, who strongly advocated group therapy. I also remembered the film *One Flew Over The Cuckoo's Nest*, which portrayed institutionalised mentally ill patients as being actually quite sane once they were able to escape from the hospital. These theories had made an impression on me and had helped to form my judgement on mental illness. Still, feeling bewildered, I could not understand how my misconceived notion of schizophrenia related to Vincent's condition.

Dr Singh listened patiently as I told him about Vincent's reluctance to be admitted to hospital or to accept medication. He told me to come back at any time and offered to give me his home telephone number. I explained that, as Vincent was at home all the time, I could not risk being caught speaking to him on the phone. I felt better after confiding in the doctor, but a little uneasy that I had also divulged details to the hospital staff in charge of my antenatal care. It felt as if I had now betrayed Vincent not once, but twice.

The following Sunday was one of the blackest days of my entire life. I thought the day would never end. After we woke up, Vincent asked me to come downstairs. He refused to let me open any curtains. Andy was awake but had strict instructions to stay upstairs until Vincent had finished talking to me. He told me to sit on the sofa. Then, suddenly and completely unexpectedly, he slammed his hand down hard repeatedly on the top of my head. With each blow, for an instant I saw a flash of white light. I was so upset and confused by his violent actions that I broke into tears. How could the husband who had been my trusting and loving protector turn into such a brutal and vicious assailant?

Vincent gave me a set of strict instructions for the day. I must not use the washing machine, the food mixer, the vacuum cleaner, the television, or the radio. No lights were to be switched on and no curtains opened all day. We were not to flush the toilet. The dogs were not to be allowed out in the garden until after dark. If I 'slipped up' at all in carrying out these instructions, I would feel his fist.

'You've been signalling to the neighbours by letting first one dog out then the other,' he said by way of accusation. 'The way you use electrical things and open the curtains is signalling to the neighbours. This house is bugged.'

I felt sorry for Andy, who was alone upstairs until Vincent had finished laying down the law. I was so relieved when he had finished his outburst and I could go upstairs to him. I also felt really sorry for the dogs, who must have felt uncomfortable all day without having the opportunity to relieve themselves. Again I felt humiliated and ashamed to be subjected to such tyranny. How much more of this could I take? I had endured over three months of this acute phase of Vincent's illness, and instead of showing signs of improvement, matters were getting worse by the day. It became inevitable now that my thoughts began to turn to leaving him. Yet I felt conflicted by the prospect of abandoning him without at least succeeding in getting him some degree of help. And if only he did get help, I thought maybe his condition would improve enough to make our life together at least tolerable.

At my next antenatal appointment with Dr Singh on the following Tuesday, feeling desperate and very distressed, I told him that I felt that I would have to leave Vincent. The doctor urged me to reconsider.

'Vincent really ought to be admitted to hospital. It can be arranged for him to come home to look after Andy while you're having the baby. If he refuses to go to hospital, he could be forced to go against his will, and the police could be used if necessary to enforce this. Is there any evidence of physical or mental cruelty to you or Andy?'

At this stage, still feeling reluctant to divulge the physical attacks, I denied any physical abuse but admitted to his mental cruelty. The prospect of a forced hospital admission aided by the police filled me with dread. Surely there had to be another way. Finally the doctor asked to see me together with Vincent at his surgery the following day. He wanted to interview us together to avoid any further reinforcement of Vincent's paranoia.

'In the meantime, make sure you don't get involved in any arguments with him,' he said. 'Be tolerant, but don't run up and down after him.'

By the time I told Vincent that Dr Singh wanted to see us together, he had already decided to stay in bed all the time. He wanted to rest but refused to eat and would drink only Coca Cola. He had no intention of getting up and was certainly not going to put himself out to see the doctor. 'If it's that important, the doctor can come here to see me at home,' he said resolutely.

Dr Singh arranged for a senior consultant to visit with him at our home and hoped that a hospital admission might result from the visit. But first he wanted to see Vincent himself, so I told him that this was okay. I had already told Vincent to expect his visit.

Dr Singh came in the morning. Vincent stayed in bed. The dogs were excited by the presence of a visitor, and the doctor seemed to have a phobia about dogs, which did not help matters. With the dogs finally under control, I showed him upstairs to the bedroom. It occurred to me that this was the first time anyone else had seen the bedroom since the work had been finished. He commented on Vincent's work as he gazed at the timber-clad ceiling, egg-shaped fireplace, and other features. I took a shoe out of Bullet's mouth and put it down, then pushed the dogs through the door so that we could talk without further distractions. Dr Singh spoke directly about the idea of Vincent being admitted to hospital. He said there was a bed for him at St Giles Hospital if he wanted it.

'I'm just physically run down,' said Vincent. 'I need a rest and a tonic.'

'He's not eating,' I added.

'You need to eat properly to regain your strength,' said the doctor.

'I'm just going to stay in bed for twenty-four hours without eating anything,' insisted Vincent.

'I don't always feel like eating either, Vincent,' I added, 'but I have to.'

The doctor then asked Vincent about his feelings about the ultrasound scans. To my surprise Vincent admitted his notion that he was somehow being affected by the scans, not that he considered that this was an admission that he was in any way deluded, of course.

'I really don't think it's possible to be affected in this way,' said Dr Singh.

'What do you know about it?' asked Vincent questioning his authority.

'I'll ask a colleague,' replied the doctor. 'He's a senior consultant who knows all about the technicalities. Can I bring him round tomorrow to visit? He's due to visit one of his patients in the area in the morning.'

Vincent agreed.

After Dr Singh had left, Vincent was annoyed with me for showing him into the bedroom. He was particularly angry about the fact that I had placed the shoe on the fireplace after I had taken it from the dog's mouth. Then he asked me to do a couple of jobs for him. 'These jobs need to be done straight away,' he said. 'I need you to hammer some nails in the ceiling where there are some missing. Then I need you to paint the inside of the fireplace with diluted sealant. There's another job, but it doesn't need to be done straight away.'

It was a struggle to reach the ceiling, but I managed to hammer the nails in as I perched precariously on the edge of the bed. Then I proceeded to do the next job. Everything had to be done according to Vincent's precise instructions. Although I did not mind doing the jobs, Vincent had me running up and down three flights of stairs time and again to fetch tools from the basement, only then to change his mind about the tools, so that I would have to go all the way down and up again. I was breathless and sweating. He gave the impression that it was taboo for him to touch anything.

The next day Dr Singh came as arranged with the consultant. This time Vincent got up out of bed and came down to the living room. Again Vincent admitted to his feelings about the scans. The consultant was very abrupt in his manner and direct with his questions. 'Have you ever felt aggressive towards your wife?' he asked.

'Yes, I've hit her a couple of times,' he admitted casually as if this was perfectly acceptable behaviour. I was utterly amazed that he admitted this. He also talked openly about an idea he had that the baby was going to be dark. It was unclear why he should expect the baby to be darker than Andy. It suggested that he thought he was not the father. Although Vincent was not very dark skinned, we had both been a little surprised by Andy's skin colour, which was only a slight shade darker than mine. His hair was light brown with loose curls.

The consultant then made it quite clear to Vincent that it was not scientifically possible for him to be affected by the ultrasound scans, or indeed by any electrical appliance in the house. He spoke with authority emphasising that he was certain of the facts. He then said that Vincent ought to be in hospital undergoing treatment. At this point, both Vincent and I asked about the nature of such treatment.

'It's simply a matter of taking medication,' replied the consultant. 'No amount of talking will make any difference.'

'Can this be arranged for me as an outpatient?' asked Vincent beginning to show signs of agitation.

'No that's out of the question,' he replied. 'You must go to hospital for the treatment.'

As Vincent became more aggressive in his manner, I sensed that the doctors were in a hurry to leave. I wanted to ask the consultant more questions, but there was no time left. He collected his coat impatiently.

'If you refuse to be admitted, I'll hand the case over to social services. I'm sorry, but we must leave. We have other patients to see.'

Both Vincent and I felt dissatisfied. Vincent was suspicious that the consultant had a file on him, even though ostensibly he had called in only as he was on his way to see another patient. He therefore knew it was more than a casual visit.

Later the same day, a young woman called Liz and a young man called Barry from social services called. Vincent let them in. They asked if they could first speak to me on my own. Vincent was annoyed at this. Although I would have welcomed the opportunity to speak to them without Vincent's menacing presence, it struck me as undiplomatic of them. As Vincent did not agree, we all sat down together.

'How are you, Mrs Adams?' they asked. 'How is your pregnancy progressing?'

'Why are you so concerned about her?' Vincent objected belligerently, cutting off my polite response as if I was stealing his thunder. The conversation then revolved around a lengthy attempt to get Vincent to agree to be admitted to hospital. In protest, Vincent's main line of argument was that, as social workers, they were not qualified to make judgements about his state of mind.

'We can assure you that we have sufficient medical evidence in our records,' they said.

'What evidence?' asked Vincent.

'The doctor who interviewed you on your first visit the emergency clinic at the hospital assessed you as suffering from the early onset of schizophrenia.'

I wondered how odd then that Vincent had come away from that interview with sleeping tablets and no notion of the serious nature of his illness. Vincent refused to accept what the social workers were telling him. 'That psychiatrist gave me the impression that there was nothing wrong with me.'

After a while, the social workers asked to be excused for a moment while they went outside for a private conversation. Then, standing by the door, they informed us of the legal implications should Vincent still refuse to be admitted. In brief, Vincent could be forcibly admitted. This outraged Vincent and alarmed me. We questioned them further to make sure we had understood correctly. Assuring us that this was not a threat but a point of information about the legal aspects, they left us to think things over. Barry said he would call in with a colleague the following day and left us some telephone numbers including a twenty-four-hour emergency service.

The next day, Friday, when they came, Vincent was busy in the kitchen chopping some frozen meat for the dogs. He insisted on finishing this before he came to talk, so we waited for him. Andy was feeling tired and miserable. We passed the time by talking about my pregnancy as they asked how I was coping. I explained that I had not had any time to dwell on the pregnancy at all; whereas, when I had been expecting Andy I had read books on pregnancy and had felt generally enthralled. Eventually Vincent joined us and explained that he did not feel ready to be admitted to hospital, as there was still work to be completed on the front of the house. They complimented Vincent on his efforts to improve the house. The new social worker, whose name was Charles, seemed much more skilled in his approach. He had a gentle sympathetic manner that inspired confidence in his professional ability and somehow made me feel protected by his calm presence. Before long he persuaded Vincent to be admitted as a voluntary patient. Perhaps by then Vincent had already half conceded to the idea after considering the prospect of an involuntary admission. Nevertheless he had thought through his terms of acceptance. He asked to have in writing an agreement that he could discharge himself at any time. This was agreed, and they asked Vincent if he was prepared to come with them straight away. I expected him to object, but after a few more questions he agreed. I could scarcely believe it.

During the discussion Andy had been acting awkwardly saying over and over again that he needed the potty but then refusing to perform in it. I could see that Vincent was getting annoyed again. He picked Andy up and turned to go upstairs with him to get ready to leave. As he did so, he pointed his finger at me and said, 'That's my problem. She's the one who's at the bottom of all this.'

I understood that he could no longer blame people at work for playing 'stunts' on him and that he needed someone else to blame. After all, if he did not blame his problem on others, he would be forced to confront the truth of the matter—that his condition was intrinsic to his own psyche. Although I knew that I had done nothing to feel guilty about, and no matter how I tried not to take his accusations personally, Vincent still managed to inflict elements of doubt on me. To my own annoyance, the tears started to flood again. The social workers passed me a box of tissues, but I told them not to fuss, explaining that I simply needed to release the tension.

Vincent came downstairs wearing his best tweed suit, which seemed inappropriate. I naturally wondered about pyjamas, toothbrush, and other toiletries but felt it best to simply let him leave in case interference on my part should prompt him to change his mind. The social worker called

Charles told me he would call in again to see me once Vincent had been admitted.

I felt a certain degree of relief but still could not quite visualise Vincent settling into a hospital environment. Andy went to sleep straight away after they left. Before long Charles returned. We sat down and talked for a while. I told him how frightening Vincent could be. For example, there had been several instances when he would pick up a tool or heavy object, hold it in front of my face, and tell me in no uncertain terms not to look down my nose at him; otherwise, he threatened, he would knock my head off my shoulders. I expressed my reservations about his ability to settle in at the hospital and stay there for treatment as he had a strong sense of independence and self-preservation which I felt was bound up with his aggression. He simply was not a passive type who would easily place his trust in others, especially when it came to tampering with his mind. I asked about the importance of talking therapy mentioning R.D. Laing and I asked for more information about the treatment. He recommended a book on schizophrenia.

'I don't know much about it, but the drug treatment seems to work,' said Charles. 'You should be aware that the theories of R.D. Laing were eventually discredited, as group therapy alone has been proven to be ineffective.'

I thanked Charles for everything and said it was a marvellous achievement to get Vincent admitted. As long as Vincent stayed in hospital, which was by no means certain, I would be able to get hold of the book, read all about this bewildering mental disorder, and hopefully I could then feel better equipped to help. On the other hand, if Vincent caught me reading about paranoid schizophrenia, I expected that he would fly into a rage. He would not tolerate the mention of the illness and was convinced that it in no way applied to him.

Now, for the first time in many months, I was able to relax at home without being hounded and stressed by Vincent's presence.

Chapter 8

Back to Square One

Vincent phoned from the hospital to ask if I could bring him some things. I packed his pyjamas, socks, underwear, and toiletries. On the way to the hospital I bought the items he requested: cigarettes, Mars Bars, and Coca Cola. I took Andy with me. We had a long walk through empty corridors and up several flights of stairs to reach the ward. Most of the old Victorian building appeared to be unoccupied. The atmosphere in the ward was friendly. There was a common room with a television, tables, and chairs. The bedrooms each had four beds separated by curtains. The décor looked dingy and depressing. Vincent unpacked the things I had brought and asked why I had packed blue socks. I wondered what possible objection he could have to that colour. He sorted out the things, handing most of the items back to me to take back home. He asked me to buy some new pyjamas and a hairbrush.

Before we left, Vincent's doctor asked to see me. Vincent had already had a long interview with her. She was an attractive young woman who was pleasant to talk to. Her name was Rita Green. She asked me about our life together from the time we had first met. I told her in some detail about the stages of our relationship that I judged to be of significance. Some of the things I had pushed to the back of my mind I was now able to view differently in the light of his illness. This included a six-month period when Vincent had been on strike from work on a matter of principle relating to health and safety, even though it had been only himself and Nigel taking strike action. During this period he had re-pointed the brickwork on the back of the house. The long periods of work on the house had included almost six months working fanatically on the bathroom. I had assumed that working into the early hours or right through the night leading to exhaustion had contributed to his illness. It was at that time that his aggression had been more acutely directed at Nigel. He had claimed that Nigel had been deliberately feigning stupidity. At work he had claimed that the other workmen were practising some form of communication among themselves without including him and that someone had been putting chemicals on his chair or in his tea. He was suspicious of people in the neighbourhood, expressed suicidal thoughts, refused to eat, and had bouts of insomnia. He made unfounded accusations about me and seemed unshakable in his beliefs, refusing to see reason. His paranoia had now centred on me, and he had recently shown a series of deluded ideas as well as inflicting mental and physical abuse.

I asked Dr Green if she had been able to reach a diagnosis.

'I need more time to be certain,' she replied.

'Is it possible to say how long Vincent needs to stay in hospital?' I asked.

'Quite a long time. First he'll have to be under observation for about two weeks. As he seems to be unwilling to accept medication, I won't prescribe anything yet. All in all I'd estimate about six weeks. He's very disturbed, but there's a lot we can do to help. The most important thing is that Vincent is going to get treatment. Without treatment his condition will continue to deteriorate.'

There were so many more questions I wanted to ask, but it had already been a time-consuming interview, and now that he was safely admitted I thought the other questions could wait. I found it difficult to keep to the point when discussing Vincent, as it was so easy to get side tracked. There was always so much to say, and the intensity of the experience made me get totally absorbed when I was relating episodes.

The thought that, without treatment, Vincent's condition could deteriorate further made me shudder. I already thought that things had reached the lowest point. Before we finished talking, I emphasised how frightening Vincent could be now that his paranoia had centred on me. She said that it would be interesting to see if, with time in hospital, his paranoia would transfer to her. Although this struck me as odd, I had already seen how Vincent's perception had shifted from seeing his boss as a father figure to a tormentor.

'Now go home and get a good night's sleep. If you think of anything else to tell me or if you simply wanted to talk, you can either call in or speak to me on the phone in the afternoons.'

I collected Andy from Vincent's room and went home. The house seemed empty. I could not get to sleep at all that night. I kept sitting up and making notes of things I had forgotten to tell Dr Green. There had been Vincent's submissive attitude following his return to work, which had seemed so out of character. I had also overlooked mentioning comments he had made about the importance of his father to him. He had told me of being severely punished as a child, and his determination never to cry whenever he had been beaten. He also had told me how he'd sensed his father's bitter disappointment in him when he'd met Vincent again. He had felt rejected by his father who had never been there for him. Yet he had never expressed any strong views about his mother or talked about her.

As I lay there that night I thought about Vincent's firm resolve to make sure that his own children would not suffer the same fate he had. Together we had agreed to allow our children's talents to develop; we would not try to push them against their will into other directions. We did not want to inflict a set of harsh rules, but we expected our children to be able to develop freely in a harmonious atmosphere. Vincent was determined to be a good parent, and he took his responsibilities very seriously. I wondered how much of this was relevant to what was happening to him, and how much of this I should share with the doctor. I could not stop turning these thoughts over in my mind. If Vincent was so determined to be a good father, how could he consider moving abroad to work? That evening when he had talked about going away, without any clear idea of where he would go or for how long, he had asked me what I would think of him. How significant was this, I wondered.

All night as I lay awake I cried a river to release the emotions which I had had to keep restrained for so long. Vincent complained if he heard me crying in bed saying that I disturbed his sleep. If I cried in the daytime when he upset me, he claimed that I was putting on an act. Sometimes when I took the dogs out to the park, I felt a strong urge to cry, but for the sake of appearances I had to choke back the tears.

One night in bed before Vincent had been admitted to hospital I had felt a desperate need for reassurance and had asked him to put his arms round me and hold me. 'You snake,' he said pushing me away and resolving never to make love to me again. 'You'll try anything, won't you!'

He thought I was making sexual advances as some kind of trap when all I simply needed was a hug. I should have realized that I would never be able to seek comfort from him for my own sorrow. He had no feelings for me and had no idea how I was being affected by his illness. It was as if we were on different planets. He could no more relate to the way I felt than I could understand the mental anguish that he was going through.

Talking to the doctor helped me to view things more clearly. I was able to recognize those trigger points that marked the onset of Vincent's more acute phases. Three distinct factors appeared to be his return to work after a long period of isolation at home, my second pregnancy with its increased burden of responsibility, and the pressure to finish the work on the house now that it was so close to completion. I hoped that I would be able to continue to gain a deeper understanding of this terrible alienating illness. For Vincent, for my sake, and for the sake of our children, I needed to know what the prospects were of a recovery.

The next day, a Saturday, I needed to buy the things that Vincent had asked for, and I needed a comfortable pair of shoes for myself for the winter. It was now the beginning of October. After my sleepless night I felt like a wreck. First I left my bag behind in one of the shoe shops when I had quickly walked out to take Andy to the toilet. Fortunately the shop assistant had looked after the bag for me. Then Andy got lost in a large stationery store, and I had to walk round calling after him feeling panic stricken. Eventually I found him wandering round looking for me, but by this time I was on the verge of tears. I scooped him up, pushed past the queue at the checkout, and ran to the car giving way to the tears. The pregnancy and lack of sleep combined with the stress made me feel very emotional and forgetful. I hated crying, as my face would go red and my eyes would look swollen, but I simply could not control it.

That evening we went to visit Vincent. He was feeling fed up and was already talking about coming home. I showed him the hairbrush I had bought, but he huffed and gave it back to me. I handed him the navy blue pyjamas but he disliked the colour and asked me to exchange them for a warmer pair in a neutral colour. His manner was very abrupt. He accepted the cigarettes but looked at me suspiciously when I explained that Andy had started to pull the cellophane wrapping off one of the packets.

To my relief, one of the nurses came in for a chat. She was incredibly patient and tolerant. She just accepted everything that Vincent said with comments such as, 'Yes, I can understand that you feel that way.' Vincent told her he felt he was wasting his time there and would not be staying much longer. Dr Green had told me that he would be forced to stay for three days to begin with because she feared for his own safety if he left. He seemed to be unaware of this. She said it was not a locked ward, but that if he tried to leave he would be called back. We sat together in the common room for a while and then Andy and I left. The next day, Sunday, we visited once more. After we reached home, Vincent phoned. 'I've decided to come home. The food here is rubbish. I've not had a check-up or been given any medicine. I think I'll be better off at home.'

He had been admitted on a Friday, and there was very little to keep the patients occupied over the weekend. Some were even allowed home. Dr Green was off duty all weekend. After Vincent's phone call, I rang the nurse to explain that Vincent was in danger of walking out if nothing was done to occupy him. Early the next morning before Dr Green came back on duty, he walked out and walked home. The three days were up. It appeared that no one had tried to persuade him to stay. I felt devastated. We were back to square one. There was a phone call from Dr Green, but Vincent made it clear to her that he had been wasting his time in hospital.

Needless to say, I felt extremely unhappy about his discharge, yet hardly surprised given Vincent's determination and the casual approach at the hospital. It had taken a time-consuming and major effort to achieve Vincent's admission. There had been a real prospect of him finally accessing treatment. I had dared to hope that he might eventually begin to show signs of improvement. Now my hopes were dashed. I had no strength in reserve to make my objections known to the authorities or to take on the entire mental health system.

Almost straight away Vincent started doing some work on the back of the house. First he re-pointed some brickwork making a thick ring of mortar round where the pipes came out of the wall. When he asked me if the work was okay, it was clear to me that he was still uncertain about what he was doing. He was still convinced that he was being watched even though he was not even visible from other houses. Then he decided to render the walls and re-coat the floor in the outside toilet. He sent me to get a new toilet seat. On the way I stopped to call Dr Green from a public call box. This was a decade before the advent of mobile phones. As she was unavailable, I spoke to a different doctor asking about the section of the law under which Vincent had been detained. He remembered Vincent and explained that there was no locked ward at that hospital. He told me the names of two other hospitals where Vincent ought to have been admitted if a bed had only been available. This was little consolation to me. I tried on several other occasions to speak to Dr Green, but without success.

On the Tuesday, I went for my antenatal appointment hoping to see Dr Singh, but unfortunately one of his relatives had died and his midwife was running his clinic. We made the arrangements for my hospital stay. I asked for a forty-eight-hour stay, and Dr Singh had arranged for his midwife to oversee the delivery of the baby. Vincent was unhappy with this. He wanted me to change to a different hospital, but I was unwilling to change, especially as I had confided in the hospital staff at the antenatal clinic. Vincent had by now developed a deep-rooted hatred for Dr Singh, holding him to blame as my accomplice for the alleged conspiracy to get him certified. In the end, to pacify Vincent, I agreed to change the arrangement with the midwife. I asked the doctor, who was now back from his leave, to put whoever happened to be on duty at the hospital maternity unit in charge of the delivery.

It took Vincent several days to complete the work in the outside toilet. He sent me to buy a flexible tap connector to replace the copper pipe in the cistern. As he had installed the present one only a few years previously, I could not understand why he wanted to replace it, but he only got annoyed if I asked him. He asked me to hold the light for him while he struggled to disconnect the fitting. He got so annoyed that he suddenly hit my hand hard with a heavy spanner leaving a big, painful bruise. This time I did not cry, but I felt a strong sense of resentment at Vincent's cruel streak. Did he really expect me to keep taking such abuse?

I began to reflect on my past three years with Vincent. I remembered the verbal abuse to which Nigel had been subjected when they had done work together on the house. It was a fact that Nigel was not very smart. For example, when Vincent had showed him the correct way to stack bricks, Nigel kept forgetting and stacking them a different way, which infuriated Vincent. When he explained to Nigel how to read a spirit level, Nigel would get confused, and as a consequence, cost Vincent a lot of time and trouble. This infuriated Vincent all the more, to the extent that he believed that Nigel was deliberately acting stupid. I never saw Vincent strike out physically at Nigel, though he got close to doing so at times. His verbal attacks were bad enough, as he humiliated Nigel sometimes to the point where he tried to make him feel the younger man owed his very existence to him. Vincent impressed on him that it had only been as a result of his own efforts that Nigel had passed his driving test, and that only by letting him live with us virtually free of rent that he was able to save enough money to buy a car.

It was therefore clear to me that Vincent was now using me as a target for his attacks. 'All you've done is go out to work and have a baby' was a typical criticism, as if these efforts were insignificant. In the same way that he felt Nigel had deliberately acted stupid to annoy him, he felt that I was provoking and pushing him to lose his temper—not overtly, but in a subtle, calculating way. His sense of alienation at work had similarly been caused by his impression that he was being provoked. By a peculiar association he had the notion that using words that contained two identical vowels was suggesting the same sign as sticking up two fingers. He also made the same interpretation if someone placed two mugs of coffee on the table. He referred to this as 'giving somebody two'. At the time I would get impatient with him when he started to refer to these weird interpretations and associations. I told him that I did not accept such practices by people, and after a while he agreed not to discuss such thoughts with me.

Unfortunately, Nigel seemed to be very impressionable. He would never challenge what Vincent told him. He laughed when Vincent laughed and did not put up any defence in the face of verbal abuse. I did not consider theirs to be a healthy relationship. When Vincent finally asked him to leave, they had been having difficulty with the tiling in the bathroom. Vincent had decided to use sand and cement rather than tile adhesive. It was tricky to get the tiles to adhere properly, as I discovered first hand when I tried to help. After working through the night to complete one section of tiling, Vincent noticed that the tiles were running out of level at the top edge through Nigel's incompetence with the spirit level. He flew into a rage and smashed the tiles. Dismissing Nigel's help as a complete hindrance, he gave him two weeks' notice to leave and find somewhere else to live. After Nigel left, it was a long time before Vincent saw him again.

I felt glad that Nigel had left, but felt bad about the circumstances. I told Vincent that I could not accept that Nigel had acted dumb deliberately to annoy him. It made no sense. It was clear to me that Nigel would be better off making a fresh start. He was only twenty-four. While he had put up with a lot from Vincent, he had relied on him too heavily instead of using his own initiative. It was time for him to move on.

Before Nigel left, while he and Vincent had been working on the kitchen, Vincent and I had reached a crisis point with one another. He had started making accusations that I was involved with a group of people who were influencing me against him. This was reminiscent of what he had told me about the cause of the breakdown of his previous marriage. He felt I was too friendly with people in the local shops. I denied all this. I was not involved with a group of people, and in the shops I was simply exchanging courtesies. He saw some strange significance in my membership in two professional associations, which I found unfathomable. I did not discuss my work with him, so had no reason to mention the professional associations. He told me I had changed my personality, which I also denied. Materially I felt I had gained a lot from our partnership, but I had not got carried away by this in the way he was suggesting. He tried to humiliate me by forcing me to wear my old glasses and keeping an old pair of shoes on display as a reminder of the kind of person I had been when we had met. He wanted me to prove my allegiance to him by taking some time off work, which I felt reluctant to do. At first I refused, but he was adamant. It became an issue to prove whether I cared more for him or my work. If I had understood more clearly at the time that he was showing signs of serious mental illness, I would probably have given in to him more readily. I felt bewildered and upset. I did not know that some of this behaviour represented the stirrings of paranoid schizophrenia. I phoned in sick and took a week off work. At around this time, some of the pupils had noticed that I was not my usual cheerful self.

At the height of this crisis in our relationship, Vincent had actually threatened divorce. This had upset me, as I had never stopped loving him. In spite of all his strange ways and his annoyance towards Nigel, I felt that we had come too far together to give up simply on account of some irritations, false impressions, and unfounded allegations. It was a time to reassess our lives and recommit. It seemed that Vincent had tried to put me to the test.

'Just what do we actually have in common with each other?' he would ask in a negative tone. At times it was difficult for me to put up a strong defence. I did not respond well to confrontation and seized up inside. Annoyed with myself, I felt that I was being too passive. I was behaving as I had witnessed Nigel respond. Feeling upset, I sometimes burst into tears, and at that time, he seemed reassured that I was expressing true emotion.

After two weeks of this turbulence came a turning point. Vincent confessed to me that he had had an affair with one of Nigel's ex-girlfriends. This came as a complete shock. He explained that I had been so bound up with my work in the evenings that he had felt excluded. The young woman had found him attractive and had apparently felt very serious about him. He had soon realized that it was foolish to carry on because he loved me and had no intention of leaving me, so he stopped seeing her. He somehow had the impression that I knew about the affair. I wondered if a troubled conscience had had some effect on his state of mind. Whatever the cause of his instability and the affair, the outcome of the crisis was to become clearer. I forgave him for the affair, and Vincent wanted us to have a much closer relationship. The most important single factor was to put one another first before all else.

After this reappraisal, we had recommitted to our relationship by deciding to start a family. Our lives for a while seemed to return to normal. Several months after the crisis had passed, I became pregnant with Andy. I still felt bothered by the accusations and lack of trust. Vincent had never retracted these. When I questioned him about it, he passed it off saying that I should have realized at the time how much stress he was under in his efforts to finish the work on the house. When I asked if he still felt that I had been conspiring with people against him, his views remained unchanged. His ideas were fixed.

'How can I prove to you that you were wrong about this? What would change your mind?' I asked.

'It's not possible,' he replied. 'As far as I'm concerned, it's a fact.'

But he seemed to have pushed it all to the back of his mind. I felt that my continued love and devotion would eventually prove to him that he had been wrong and soften his hard-boiled attitude. With Vincent's eventual agreement, I also took out a modest life insurance policy on myself hoping that this would show additional evidence that I cared for him and put him first. Vincent had already taken out an insurance policy on his life. I also promised to reduce the amount of time I spent on my work in the evenings.

The difference now, three years later, was that Vincent seemed to be going over the edge and was unable to control his temper. Previously he had never talked about suicide or resorted to violence, and he appeared to be able to channel his extreme feelings into his work as if the creative outlet resolved his issues. Sometimes I wondered if, by working, he was managing to actively clear his head and get things out of his system. In particular the bathroom stood as a kind of monument to this.

Now, however, after his return home from the hospital, he was utterly convinced that I was again conspiring against him. His sense of alienation was so strong that I, the only person in the whole world who cared about him, appeared to him as his worst enemy. My hopes that his fixed ideas might change for the better over time were to be unanswered. He would sometimes look at me in his accusing way. 'And don't think for a moment that I've forgotten about you and your associations.' What he failed to grasp was that the only thing preventing us from becoming closer in our relationship was not other people, not my work, not his work, but his own distorted paranoid view of the world. The renewed commitment to one another, which we had made three years previously, no longer seemed valid on several counts.

After completing the work in the outside toilet, Vincent spent several days re-pointing more brickwork and fitted more air-bricks, taking care to fill the adjacent holes as he had done before. He spent a great deal of time and effort on jobs around the house that seemed to me to be futile. For example, he removed the glass shelf in the alcove in the bathroom which he had taken great care to insert only a few months previously. He became obsessed with the notion of having made mistakes in the work he had originally done and was anxious to correct them. Moreover he felt that these mistakes were somehow being pointed out to him. He snapped at me for leaving things lying around, claiming that they were on display to people coming into the house and that I was trying to indicate something to him.

Although I found all this disturbing, I felt that I needed to bide my time until my next opportunity to try to get him psychiatric help and also until after the baby was born. At least I felt there had been some degree of progress in my own understanding of his illness. This made me feel more certain of myself and a little less confused. I was slowly beginning to gain more strength in my capacity to resist his onslaughts of abuse. I was somehow less sensitive to his treatment of me.

As for signs of further deterioration in Vincent's state of mind, it now became apparent that he was hearing voices, something which disturbed me deeply, as I simply could not find any way to understand this. Vincent claimed that various people had called him names. But the names were not proper names or words but sounds such as 'la la' and 'ee ee'. He had previously claimed that people at work had used the terms towards him in a pejorative way. Now he claimed that Dr Singh had called him an 'ee ee', which I understood to mean something like an idiot or a lunatic. It made me feel quite sick to hear him talk such gibberish. I told him that the doctor had said no such thing, and that these were meaningless terms, but I realized it was pointless to try to convince him.

On one evening that week Vincent wanted me to hold the torch again for him while he finished a job. Suddenly the torchlight went out, and I could not make it come back on. It must have been the batteries or a loose connection. Vincent was livid and accused me of tampering with it to cause him aggravation. I explained to him, as I had done so many times before, that any aggravation I caused him was sure to rebound on me several times over so it made no sense to accuse me. He simply refused to accept this logical reasoning. He failed to understand how much I was affected by his anger.

Vincent then went through a black-and-white phase. After he had painted the walls of the outside toilet white and chosen a black toilet seat, this became an obsession. He painted the labels in the centre of one of his favourite albums by the Blue Oyster Cult white (presumably because of the colour blue in the name), also, for no obvious reason, he applied white paint the edge of one shelf and even to the inside of the dustbin.

His next obsession was clearing spaces and throwing things away. After clearing cupboards and storage spaces, he started a thorough clearance of the loft space above the bathroom, which consisted mainly of materials such as paint, nails, and rope, as well as roofing supplies and other building materials. A lot of this was bulky and unnecessary to keep, but not all of it. Then he started on the kitchen cupboards, showing annoyance that I had organized the contents my own way. He also became so paranoid about my cooking that he decided to cook the dinner himself every evening for a few days in succession. The meat had to be fresh, not frozen, even though the freezer was well stocked. He made the decisions about what we would eat and the way it was to be cooked.

And so he reorganized the entire contents of the kitchen cupboards and would get annoyed if ever I put something in a different place. He also started to throw away a number of items which I wanted to keep, including gifts from my family as well as things I rarely used such as a mincer and some spare jugs. He complained that the whole house was cluttered with rubbish, which from my point of view was not true at all. Following this he proceeded to rearrange the furniture in the living room. After that he started on my clothes. Many of the items he wanted to throw out happened to be blue: my old jacket, his welding machine, and his Workmate bench, which had been a gift from me, as well as two large willow-pattern oval plates, which he had bought for me. Even Andy's little bike. Whenever I objected he looked me hard in the face with eyeball confrontation. 'They've got to go!'

Eventually both rooms in the basement were piled with 'rubbish'. Just when the time came for them to be cleared out and we were prepared to load the car, there was a knock at the door. It was two women from social services. Vincent asked them in, and they sat down. They began by asking how I was. This again annoyed Vincent intensely as he felt they were supposed to be concerned with his welfare rather than mine. Vincent dominated the conversation, scarcely letting me speak. They obviously wanted to hear my views. All I could say was that I was okay and that any pressure they put on Vincent would have an adverse effect, causing him more aggravation, which would make him aggressive. I must have come across as terribly brow beaten. But at the point where Vincent claimed that the problem was no more than a marital conflict, I simply had to speak my mind. I flatly opposed this and wondered if Vincent believed this or was consciously distorting the truth. They asked if there was anything they could do to help.

'You can help to clear the rubbish from the basement if you like,' said Vincent sarcastically, giving the impression that he was a very busy man and that they were preventing him from getting on with his work.

After they had left, I helped Vincent to carry the heavy items to the car. Vincent soon became suspicious of the items I chose to carry, probably thinking that I was communicating with the neighbours. He began to get abusive towards me. The final item was a glass-panelled door, which Vincent smashed violently, sending glass flying all over the place. I had grown accustomed to his humourless way of doing things and followed his directions by helping to clean up the mess. That way any friction was kept to a minimum. I hoped that, by keeping a low profile and accepting my subservient role, somehow all this clearing process might do Vincent some good. However the cost of replacing some of the items he had insisted on throwing out concerned me. Vincent was not claiming all his sickness benefit, and it was difficult to see how we were going to manage financially. Some of the items had sentimental value. When he had asked me to sort out our collection of photographs, there were hardly any I wished to part with. There were my folders of schoolwork including translation passages. I had taken a long time to check them for accuracy with native speakers. I planned to keep them in the loft expecting that they would still be useful once I had returned to teaching.

'Don't get any ideas about going back to work,' he shouted at me. 'You're staying at home whether you like it or not.'

'I want to stay at home,' I responded. 'We agreed this. You don't need to dictate to me like that.'

What kind of a tyrant had he turned into? Previously we had always discussed things together and reached agreement without any need for him to dominate. As my confidence grew, I felt more inclined to put up some resistance from time to time. Once, after he had made further allegations that I was deliberately trying to annoy him, I simply walked away and started to go upstairs. He came after me in a rage, grabbed me by the collar of my bathrobe, and pulled it tight round my neck. I thought he was going to strangle me. He was so strong. I felt terrified and helpless in his clutches.

'It's lucky for you that you're pregnant,' he said easing his grip. 'Otherwise you might not be alive. I can quite understand these stories you hear about husbands murdering their wives.' And leaving me with that comforting thought, he let go of me.

Every time he behaved like this to me, I felt like grabbing Andy and making a run for it. However, I was well aware that to do so would be too dangerous and not worth the risks. By the time I waited for things to calm down, the feeling of panic subsided. The house was my home as well as his. If the support systems for me were anything like what I had witnessed in terms of help for Vincent, there was a huge risk that such an escape plan would go badly wrong. I kept convincing myself that his aggression would not surface again and that things would start to improve. There was a child to consider, and soon there would be a second child—a newborn baby. This put me in such a vulnerable position.

All the same, whenever I went out, I would sometimes hesitate before returning home. Vincent was beginning to become suspicious of me taking Andy out with me, probably suspecting that we might not come back. Vincent knew that I could never leave him without taking Andy. A couple of times he packed a case threatening to leave. Now I simply wished that he would go, except that he thought of taking Andy with him. Each time he backed down, and I realized he was only bluffing. I had taken so much from Vincent by now that it would have been a relief for him to leave.

I worried about the situation at home when the time would come for me to have the baby. I spoke to my mother on the phone about every two months, but could not possibly tell her what was going on. It would have given her a mental breakdown. Besides, my parents were due to go on holiday to Spain for two months. All I could do was ask my mother if she would be prepared to come and stay if it proved absolutely necessary because Vincent was unwell. She agreed without asking too many questions. This gave me some peace of mind. I had not been in contact with my sister for several months. Sometimes I would wonder how she would react if I suddenly appeared on her doorstep with Andy and the baby due imminently. I had not told her anything either. My hometown where they lived was over a hundred miles away. What could she do to help from such a distance when she had two children of her own and a busy job?

I struggled to try to put into perspective the seven years that Vincent and I had spent together. Had I been denying that I had made a gigantic mistake by marrying him? Would it become increasingly difficult to make the break as time passed? I felt compelled to leave him, but the thought was so new to me that I needed to figure out the thousand and one implications. The children had to come first before my emotional response, any practical considerations, or any concern for Vincent. What about the cat and the dogs? Should I take the car? Should I go to my sister's? What about the birth in the midst of all this uncertainty?

Later on I was able to realize that seven or eight years in an average life expectancy of seventy or eighty years was a relatively short episode, but when I was caught up in the immediacy of everything, it seemed like a long, long time. In just a couple of days I was due to turn thirty-four, still young enough to start afresh, possibly even remarry. I needed to make up my mind whether to make the break before Andy was old enough to be affected by being uprooted. I was concerned that he might already feel the effects of the tensions at home. I just did not feel quite yet prepared to do it. I was determined to try one last time to get Vincent medical help. It was the least I could do. We had come too far for me to desert him. He had sacrificed so much to provide us with a home. I still had feelings for him. He was so misguided by his illness that he did not realize what he was doing to me.

Such was the nature of the conflict I felt. After things had calmed down again I asked Vincent a question which had obviously been on my mind. 'When you told me I was lucky to be pregnant, what about after the baby's been born? What then?'

'You'll just have to take a chance' was his callous and chilling reply.

Chapter 9

The Second Attempt to Section

The time came for my next hospital appointment. As had been promised, I saw the same sister and doctor, Dr Wardle, I had seen at the previous appointment. I told them about Vincent's weekend in hospital. It felt so comforting to be able to talk again to someone. They were very concerned, especially when I told them I had been thinking more and more about leaving home. Dr Wardle would not hear of it. 'This is no time to talk about leaving home. Your baby could be born any day now. If it comes to the worst and you feel like leaving home, come here. We can admit you early. Fortunately the wards are not full at the moment.'

I felt overwhelmed by his kind offer. Although it was only a couple of days short of my original expected date of confinement, I did not feel any sign that the birth was imminent. I did not expect to need to take up the offer of an early admission. Yet it helped enormously to know that the offer was open.

Dr Wardle felt strongly that Vincent should be readmitted. He was anxious to help to make the arrangements for another home visit with this aim in mind. He asked me to wait while he phoned the social services department. It was a fairly long wait. I wondered how I was going to explain my delay in arriving home to Vincent. I decided to say that I had stayed to take a look round the maternity wards and that the sister did actually give me a quick look round before I left the hospital. I was surprised that there were so many empty beds. I felt happy to be going there to have the baby. It was much friendlier than the bigger hospital where Andy had been born. The doctor reappeared saying that he had made the arrangements with the social services, and that I could expect a phone call at home in the afternoon. I thanked him and rushed home.

Vincent did not question my excuse for taking longer than usual. I told him about my visit to the maternity wards and favourable impressions. I felt a bit uneasy about things being taken out of my hands by the health care staff. When the phone rang, it was the less experienced social worker called Barry. He asked me if Vincent was there. I said, 'Yes.' He asked me to answer each of his questions with a simple yes or no. I agreed but knew that Vincent would catch on and start to get suspicious.

'For the moment are you okay?'

'Yes.'

'Is Vincent still acting aggressively and threatening you?'

'Yes.'

'Will you be able to contact me or call in to see me tomorrow morning as a result of the doctor's request for another home visit?'

'Yes, okay.'

As predicted, Vincent was unsettled by the phone call and asked what the social worker had wanted. I said he had just asked if we were both okay and if Vincent was still busy working on the house.

'All he needs to do is ask you to answer a load of questions and ask you to say yes or no,' he said, reading the situation perfectly well. I realized that I had to be careful. I did not feel at all confident about the situation.

The next day I went to the optician's and called in at the social services offices nearby. I was shown into an interview room. When Barry came in, I told him how apprehensive I felt about another home visit. 'Vincent is no fool,' I told him. 'He is suspicious at the best of times and will immediately assume the visit to be yet another attempt to get him admitted to hospital. I can't imagine him cooperating as he did before.'

'Mrs Adams, you must appreciate that Vincent is suffering from an acute illness, and this really is the only way to get him readmitted. You know that, if necessary, police assistance will be called upon.'

'Vincent has already threatened that, if ever the police came to take him away, he will get to me first, before they even have a chance to set foot through the door.'

'Do you think that you could find an excuse to go out and take Andy with you so that you can be out of the house at the time the visit is planned?'

'I'll do my best, but I can't be certain that this will work.' I paused to search for a better way to approach the problem, then I asked, 'Is there any way that Vincent can be sectioned while attending an outpatient visit with Dr Green?'

'This is not possible for two reasons,' Barry pointed out. 'First there must be no deception, and second the procedure strictly requires the assessment visit to take place in the patient's home. Just be careful and leave the house if you can. If there's any danger, go straight to the Homeless Families Unit. They have everything there you'll need if you don't have chance to take anything with you.'

'I still can't get used to the idea of leaving home,' I said. 'At the moment I don't feel that separation or divorce is the right solution.'

'It's useful to know this,' he commented looking surprised and added glibly, 'The vast majority of cases like these end in separation or divorce.'

Reluctantly I agreed to phone him after I had managed to get out of the house with Andy. I wondered why both Dr Singh and Dr Wardle had advised me not to leave Vincent. I expected it was because the birth was imminent and because they held out hope that, with treatment, Vincent's condition could improve.

The next day, again a Friday, I waited for my opportunity to go out after Vincent had kept me busy with one thing after another. I normally went to the supermarket to do the weekly food shopping. Vincent kept telling me that it could wait. He had decided to paint the radiators in the basement. The phone rang, and I went upstairs to answer it. It was someone from social services asking if I was okay and saying that Dr King, Vincent's preferred doctor from the group practice, would call in at about eleven o'clock, followed by a visit by a senior psychiatrist and finally some social workers. In a quiet voice I told the woman on the phone that I had not been able to leave the house and that Vincent was very suspicious. She told me that I would be able to leave with the social workers if I wished. While I understood the need to avoid deception, I was afraid that Vincent might not let any of them in or that he might react violently to the visits. Unable to tell the truth, I told him that the call was from the education office asking if I could tell them if or when I was planning to go back to work. He must have sensed that something was brewing. I felt very on edge.

At eleven o'clock the doorbell rang so I quickly went upstairs from the basement, but Vincent ran upstairs after me reaching the door just as I opened it to let Dr King in.

'You were expecting me, weren't you?' said Dr King. My heart sank. Vincent knew I had lied to him. I evaded the question, and Vincent asked Dr King point blank the reason for his visit.

'Because they think you should be inside again' was the doctor's reply. An unfortunate way of putting it, I thought. 'I mean, in hospital,' he said, rephrasing his words. 'How are you feeling?'

'Fine,' replied Vincent.

Dr King asked Vincent if he was working and asked him several other questions to which Vincent gave abrupt, single-word responses. It was clear that he had no intention of cooperating. Then, turning to me, Vincent said, 'She's the one who's sick and ought to be in hospital.' I felt powerless. I lost all confidence. The situation felt hopeless. As much as I wanted to appear to be strong, calm, and composed, I could not manage to hold back the choking tears.

'Why is she crying?' Dr King asked Vincent. This doctor always managed to unnerve me. I found his manner arrogant and dismissive. I always felt that I was floundering in an attempt to find the right words. Surely as a doctor he should know that pregnancy hormones affect the ability to control emotion. Feeling as if I had reached rock bottom and had nothing left to lose, I plucked up the courage to speak. 'I feel at risk. Vincent has been behaving very strangely, and I feel frightened of him.'

'Has he hurt you?' asked Dr King.

'Yes. He has hit me hard on the head,' I replied forgetting to mention the partial attempt to strangle me and the blow to my hand with the spanner. I simply lacked the presence of mind. I had not prepared any answers and had hoped that I would be safely out of the house during this visit.

'What is it about his behaviour that you consider to be abnormal?' he asked.

'He keeps going over the work to the house that he'd already completed,' I replied feeling that this was not the best example. It was really difficult to talk about all the things while Vincent was present defending himself on every point that I raised and making out that this was simply a domestic crisis. It was also particularly difficult because I knew he would unleash his anger on me afterwards. It was obvious that he was absolutely furious with me, and Dr King probably sensed his anger too, as he walked towards the door and left in a hurry.

Vincent was outraged.

'Why did you lie to me? Why?'

'I was trying to help you,' I said, feeling worthless and scared.

First he dragged me upstairs and tore my dress off. He put his hands round my neck in a stranglehold. Then he hit my face hard knocking my glasses to the floor. Andy was still downstairs, so thankfully was spared from witnessing this scene. Vincent went down to him and told him everything was okay. Eventually I nervously changed my clothes and went downstairs. I admitted that I had deceived him, but tried to explain that it was only in the interest of getting him help. He was already utterly convinced that I had been deceiving him in so many other ways. I insisted that this was the only time, explaining that I was afraid that he would not let the doctor in if he had known that he was going to visit. I tried to put my arms round him as a way of showing that I was sorry, but he did not want to hold me.

'Look. Don't try to help me!' he implored me in a thundering tone, pointing his finger in my face.

We went back down to the basement, and he decided to clean all the fresh paint off the radiators. He made me help, even though I was still in floods of tears.

Before long the next visitor arrived. This time I answered the door before Vincent had a chance to come upstairs. It was the senior consultant psychiatrist who was standing in for the one who had visited on the first attempt to get Vincent admitted. I told him straight away that Vincent had attacked me after Dr King's visit and that I would not be able to stay in the house after this visit.

Vincent appeared, and the consultant introduced himself. He asked Vincent to sit down so that they could talk. Vincent refused. Again he turned to me, calling me a snake. The consultant asked if he could talk to Vincent alone, so I took Andy and started to go back downstairs planning to head straight for the front door in the basement. Vincent immediately suspected my move and refused to let us go.

'Give me a cheque for half the money in the bank. I'm leaving,' he said. I kept my chequebook in the basement, so I continued downstairs, not stopping to think whether I should give him the cheque. As I was halfway down the stairs Vincent pushed me hard from behind, causing me to fall backwards catching my back on the steps.

'Oh! You tripped!' he callously called out loud enough for the consultant to hear. How I hated him for that.

Without any concern for the consultant upstairs, he unleashed his anger on me yet again with more blows to the head and face. Then he went back upstairs and ordered the consultant out of the house, telling the social workers who had gathered on the front steps exactly what he thought of them as well.

I thought the consultant must have heard enough to be alarmed for my safety. I had told him quite clearly that I could not stay in the house. I had told Dr King that I felt at risk. By now it should already have been documented that Vincent had hit me on previous occasions, as he had even admitted this before. I was nine months pregnant. I therefore expected the police to arrive at any moment and enforce Vincent's compulsory admission. I sat down on the sofa, shaking uncontrollably, unable to do anything. Vincent eventually calmed down and also seemed to be waiting for the next move. Nothing happened. No further visits. No police. All was quiet. Andy had fallen asleep. I realized it would be impossible to leave the house with him. After about an hour of waiting, as it was still daylight, I said I would take the Bullet to the park before it started to get dark.

'Please yourself. Whatever's gonna happen will happen anyway,' said Vincent. So I picked up the keys.

'Not the car keys,' said Vincent, still one step ahead, obviously suspecting that I would drive off and not come back. So I took the house keys and stepped outside leaving Andy sleeping peacefully. I could handle only one dog right now, so Bailey would have to stay at home. I looked up the road expecting to see a police van, but there was no sign of any police vehicle. As I walked a short distance into the park, I felt I needed to sit down and think. I realized it was almost evening surgery hours. I went straight to the doctor's and rang the bell. Dr King answered, so I announced myself on the intercom.

'Yes, what do you want?' he asked abruptly.

'I'd like to speak to you,' I replied, amazed at his question.

He came to the door and looked at the dog. 'You can't come in here with that.'

'Now look, Dr King. This is my only chance to get out of the house. Please let me come in.'

'Oh, all right. You'll have to put the dog in the yard.'

The poor animal. He had been subjected to all this trauma and now, not only had he been cheated out of his walk, but he had to be isolated.

The doctor was in the reception area at the back of the building where the secretary also worked. She already had some idea of my difficult situation after seeing me come to talk to Dr Singh in a distressed state between patients. I asked Dr King what he had concluded from his visit.

'It appears to me to be no more than a marital upset. I can scarcely certify your husband on those grounds.'

'Had you looked at the case notes before the visit?' I asked, feeling shocked at his conclusion.

'I've just returned from holiday leave. I haven't had a chance. How did Vincent react to my visit?'

I could not think straight. I felt completely thrown and betrayed by his lack of concern. I should have said exactly how Vincent had reacted. Instead, all could think about was how impossible it was for me to return home.

'In that case I'll hand you over to social services,' he said, obviously tired of having to deal with me. He made the call, and I spoke to a woman I had never met who had been put in charge of the case. She explained that no forced admission would be possible without medical backing from the visiting doctors. I ended the phone conversation by telling her I did not feel it was the right thing to do to make myself homeless.

'What was the consultant's conclusion?' I asked Dr King.

'The same as mine. Marital conflict. Now, if you don't mind, I have other patients to see.'

This defied belief. My mouth dropped open in staggering shock and disgust.

'Don't you consider this to be an urgent matter?' I asked in desperation, feeling that he was to a great extent responsible for my predicament. 'Vincent is completely paranoid, deeply disturbed with deluded ideas, and he hears voices. He's been in hospital where this has been verified, and he discharged himself. Today he had me in a stranglehold, ripped my dress, and broke my glasses when he hit me across the face. I've been the target of physical violence several times.'

I gave a few other poignant examples of his disturbed behaviour, finally finding the flow of points that had evaded me in the presence of this doctor previously. I explained why I had been unable to speak freely when Vincent was present. Was it of no consequence that I was in the advanced stage of pregnancy and being attacked?

At this point, to my immense relief, Dr Singh walked in. I suddenly remembered Dr Wardle's offer that I could be admitted early to the maternity unit. Immediately Dr Singh rang the maternity unit and called an ambulance for me, which was expected in about half an hour. I asked Dr King if he would call Vincent and ask him to collect the dog. Dr Singh took my blood pressure, which amazingly was normal. I suggested that I should tell Vincent that I had felt faint in the park and found my way to the surgery to be checked. This was very close to the truth. Dr Singh put hypertension as the reason for my early admission, also true in a nonmedical sense, although my blood pressure was normal.

After Dr King went into his surgery, the secretary, who fortunately was a dog lover, was kind enough to fetch Bullet inside and give him a drink of water. Vincent told Dr King on the phone that he refused to collect him. I really did not want to go back to the house myself. As no one was in a position to help, I asked a boy in the street if he would be good enough to take the dog up to the front door, open the door with my key, let the dog in, and bring the keys back to me. He agreed. He came back still holding Bullet on the lead but without the keys and said that Vincent had snatched the keys out of his hand and refused to take the dog in. I went back to the doctor's with Bullet. The secretary rang her son and asked if he would take Bullet to the house, but this led to the same refusal. Then as the ambulance arrived, her husband came, and I agreed reluctantly to let him tie Bullet by his lead to the front door. Surely Vincent would take him inside this time.

It seemed that, at each stage of this second attempt to get Vincent admitted to hospital, things had gone from bad to worse. I had had my reservations about the procedures and had anticipated Vincent's refusal to cooperate as well as the backlash which he had inflicted on me. It confirmed my own distrust, knowing that professional people are simply doing a job, and that as part of this they changed shifts, had weekends free, took holiday leave, took time off, changed jobs, and had others appointed either to deputise for them or to replace them. Some lacked experience, and others lacked commitment. It was so far from adequate. Yet I had also encountered children who recognized my desperation and were willing to help me. I understood that certain professional people may have been unable to gain a complete overview of the situation through no fault of their own.

In spite of the obvious failings of others, the experience I had just been through left me feeling deeply disappointed in myself. My self confidence was shattered. I had lacked the presence of mind to speak out when it mattered, and I had lacked the ability to remain strong. The outcome of this succession of blunders, lack of support, and misfortune was that there was a collective failure to get Vincent the help that he so badly needed. As a consequence, the welfare of our whole family was now very much in the balance. It was a gross understatement to say that it felt as if all the odds were stacked against me in this attempt to find treatment of any kind, not to mention an eventual recovery. And to top it all, this impenetrable insidious psychological condition was itself feeding Vincent's aggression, alienation, and determination to refuse help.

Chapter 10

A Baby Sister for Andy

The maternity unit felt like a real haven. I felt so safe and protected. The nursing staff and doctors were sympathetic and very friendly. I had so much on my mind that I felt a compulsion to talk. The first night I could not sleep at all. My neck felt stiff and tender and my face, head, and back felt bruised. The nursing staff took note of the bruises. I cried a lot and tried to write down details of some of the things that I had found particularly disturbing about Vincent. I felt worried about leaving Andy, and I wondered if Bullet was okay. After what Dr Green had said about the possible transfer of paranoid feelings, I was concerned in case Andy became a target, if this was possible. He was left alone with Vincent, and I was no longer there to shoulder any blame. What if Vincent lost patience with him?

Apparently, on the evening when I had been admitted to the maternity unit, a welfare officer had called in at the house. She had reported that everything seemed to be okay. She forgot to ask about Bullet, so in the morning I rang Vincent to find out about him.

'No, I didn't take him in' was his response. 'That should be on your conscience.'

I was uncertain whether to believe him. I then called the police station to see if Bullet had been picked up as a stray. It was not until midday that the staff nurse came with the news that the doctor's secretary had kindly taken Bullet home with her. I rang her straight away to thank her. What a marvellous lady. She explained that she already had a dog of her own. This was why she had felt unable to offer to take Bullet at first. Then she had passed our house at eight o'clock in the evening and taken pity on the dog, who was still sitting shivering outside the front door.

I simply could not comprehend how Vincent could have left him there. Bullet had always been his favourite pet. He had shown him real affection. Yet recently he had talked often about it being wrong to show sentiment. He seemed to assume that I thought the same way. A few weeks ago, when he had been busy clearing items out of the house, he had decided to get rid of his tropical fish. The tank of fish had been in the basement flat since I had first met Vincent. I had found it a chore to clean out the tank and felt I had enough to contend with, so I agreed. I suggested taking them back to the pet shop, but Vincent was adamant about pouring them down the drain, which struck me as cruel. I felt upset to see them wriggling and struggling in the cold dirty drain water as he lowered them in the fishnet. When he realized they could not survive, he agreed to let me take them to the pet shop. I drove, still upset at the disturbing sight and Vincent's lack of emotion, to a shop and handed them over. How could he have imagined they would survive?

Now that I was resting in hospital, I had some precious time to reflect on everything. My thoughts turned to Vincent's inability to see my point of view. In our early years together it had been so different. He had been considerate, chivalrous, and protective towards me. Certain changes in him had seemed gradual over the years. The violent outbursts marked a relatively sudden change. I wondered how he could go from one extreme to another, from being so protective to being so extremely aggressive. One thing was quite clear in my mind: no matter how much he had thought I had betrayed him, I could not accept the fact that he had smacked Andy so hard, punishing him for no reason. Equally unacceptable to me was the fact that he had pushed me on the stairs, especially when I was in an advanced stage of pregnancy. It was quite bad enough that he had hit me and gripped me in a stranglehold. No, no matter how his aggression and cruelty might be in some way be symptomatic of his illness, I simply could not forgive him for this. I recalled that Dr Green had told me that only a tiny minority of patients with paranoid schizophrenia were aggressive and prone to violent outbursts. The majority were, by all accounts, simply very confused people.

After lunch I decided to ask if I could go out to the shop to buy some toothpaste and a toothbrush. I also treated myself to a bar of chocolate, as it occurred to me that it was my birthday. That evening a new patient called Sandra moved into the room opposite mine with her newborn baby. We quickly made friends. I was able to help her, as she had had a difficult delivery and it was painful for her to move about. When she told me that she used to work as a social worker, I decided to tell her the reason I had been admitted early. When I had told the nurses about Vincent's attacks, they reacted with horror and disbelief. Sandra had obviously heard many similar stories before. Nothing seemed to shock her. She said it was better for Vincent to work out his aggression rather than internalise his feelings and become vegetative like some mentally ill patients that she had visited. This made me wonder if I was in any way overreacting. She advised me to work on our relationship, which was also the advice given by one of the staff nurses.

Clearly people were trying to be helpful by giving advice based on their expertise and experiences, but I really had to be very careful to fully evaluate this advice. After all, I was the one caught up in the tangled mess, and only I had the overview of my own situation. I still wished I could gain a better understanding of schizophrenia. Dr Green had told me that the term covered a wide range of symptoms, which varied according to the individual patient. Chronic schizophrenia, for example, was a long-term illness which, as I understood it, left the patient feeling extremely lethargic. Vincent's illness appeared to be acute paranoid schizophrenia, which led to bouts of hyperactivity and had a more optimistic outlook. Apparently treatment for acute schizophrenia proved to be more effective and could be controlled to some degree, helping many patients to lead a reasonably normal life.

It struck me how quick witted Vincent had been. Maybe this was a good sign in relation to potential treatment. He had certainly been one step ahead of me when the succession of assessment visits had taken place. He had successfully negotiated his own discharge at the first attempt to avoid a hospital stay. In fact, on the second attempt it appeared that he had actually managed to convince Dr King and the senior psychiatrist that I was the one with all the problems. It surprised me that, in the company of others, he could appear to behave rationally, especially when it was a matter of great importance to him. He was obviously growing wiser with each attempt to avoid admission to hospital. I appreciated how tricky it must be to diagnose his condition. In many respects the symptoms of his illness kept morphing and at times became almost completely invisible, especially to outsiders.

I decided to phone Dr King to explain in greater detail more aspects of Vincent's behaviour that had caused me anxiety. By referring to my notes I was able to be more specific and feel more assertive. I would not give him the opportunity to redirect the conversation or cut me short until I had finished what I had to say. I began by explaining how distressed I had been feeling the day before his visit and how my pregnancy made control over my tearfulness impossible. I mentioned Vincent's threats to kill me, his attack on me after the visits by medical specialists to assess his mental state, and examples of bizarre notions such as associations between colours and his insistence on throwing away items of value. At this point he interrupted me saying that he would visit Vincent again at a later date, but that for the moment, if I agreed, we should 'let sleeping dogs lie'. Accepting this for the moment, I gave my agreement. The expression 'let sleeping dogs lie' seemed less than appropriate, particularly in view of Vincent's aggression and the turbulence caused by it. After this conversation, I felt that I had come some way towards redeeming myself, even though the outcome regarding treatment for Vincent may have remained the same, at least for the time being.

Still preoccupied by the situation, I tried to make some sense out of Vincent's reactions. It seemed that when he looked at me it was not so much me that he saw, but what I represented. He often commented on the differences between us as if these constituted irreconcilable extremes. I was white and British. He had been born in Jamaica of mixed heritage. As a teacher, I automatically belonged to the professional class, whereas, as a carpenter, he identified strongly with the working class. By nature I was quiet, gentle, and reflective. I was more of an introvert. He was talkative, confrontational, and assertive at best. During the most acute phase of his illness, he was threatening and extremely aggressive. At his worst, he was violent and outright dangerous. He viewed the world as a hostile place. I saw it as place full of trust.

Childhood for my sister and me had been carefree and mostly spent outdoors playing, left to our own devices. From a very young age, my sister and I would go off on our scooters to the bluebell woods, play in the grounds of the local chapel, make camp fires, build dens, explore cemeteries, and play games with all the other children out in the street. When it snowed we would make slides and go sledging, only coming home when we could scarcely feel our hands and feet. We walked to and from school together from the earliest age, as both our parents worked. In those days, children were afforded complete freedom to roam, unaware of potential danger and well away from the supervision of anxious parents.

At the age of eight, Vincent had been wrenched away from his familiar home with his grandmother in Jamaica. He had a very hard time seeking his father's approval and struggling to make his way as a young man. Vincent and I had started out united in love with common dreams of a future together. It had been his personal qualities that I had found so attractive. The changes in his personality had been gradual. Between isolated episodes when he had displayed negative traits, he had always reverted to the original Vincent whom I recognised. Now we had become alienated from one another and polarised. There were times when I nostalgically yearned for the man I had married. A few times I would express these feelings to him. 'The reason I keep trying to help you get treatment is so that we can get back to normal.'

'There is no normal,' he would reply. 'Things will never be the same as before.'

I seriously wondered if my stable background and the love I felt for him would be strong enough to make any kind of impact in view of his illness, his refusal of treatment, and his intransigent attitude, as well as his background and upbringing. But I still felt determined to try.

It had seemed impossible to get Vincent to see reason. He had worked out in his misguided perception that my ultimate motive was to get the house for myself. He saw this all as an attempt to break him down. Moreover he had told me that he suspected that I had an accomplice. He actually thought that I was having an affair. I found this such a ridiculous notion. I was completely under Vincent's domination, nine months pregnant, looking after a two-year-old, and had neither inclination nor opportunity to have an affair. It had never crossed my mind to be unfaithful to him. Yet he talked about this fictitious idea as if it were an absolute fact.

Another obsession that I gave a lot of thought to was Vincent's conviction that I was competing against him. He felt that I was flaunting the little knowledge I had of building work, which he had passed on to me. He also felt that people, myself included, resented his skills and talents and that this resentment prompted us to persecute and ridicule him. This was a real persecution complex. When he had been uncertain about his work and had asked for my advice, he had claimed that I gave him the wrong advice, deliberately, to mislead him.

There was no psychiatry department at the hospital where I had been admitted. One of the doctors in the maternity unit, Dr Walker, told me that she knew Dr Green at St Giles, the psychiatric hospital. I talked to her quite a lot. Both she and Dr Wardle were of the opinion that the birth of the baby would mark a turning point. They thought that Vincent's mental state would either start to improve or reach a crisis point, in which case he could be readmitted for treatment, if necessary by being sectioned.

I thought long and hard about the long-term effects of a forced admission. With his track record of holding me responsible for so many things that I had clearly not done, it seemed inevitable that he would blame me in the event of any forced admission to hospital. With his stubborn beliefs, even in the face of clearly misguided events, the blame would be etched firmly in his mind, never to be forgotten, re-evaluated, or forgiven. I felt alone with the burden of weighing up all these factors, forecasts, opinions, and pieces of advice. I had been given no real advice on this matter by a psychiatrist.

As I was still concerned about Bullet, I phoned the doctor's secretary at the group practice to check if he was behaving himself. She told me not to worry and said the family had grown very fond of him. My heart warmed to this news. However, I still felt it was an imposition. I needed to ask Vincent if he would take the dog back home.

After a day or two, the sister rang Vincent and asked if he could bring some things for me. He came with Andy, who climbed all over my bed exploring every gadget hanging on the wall. I felt so pleased to see him.

'We're not staying long,' said Vincent.

'Can you bring my knitting the next time you come?' I asked.

'How long are you going to be in here?'

'They're waiting for some test results,' I replied, knowing full well that I would be staying until after the baby was born.

They visited again the following day and brought me the things I had asked for. When I went to the toilet, Andy followed me. Vincent began to look worried as if this was a carefully planned plot to snatch Andy away from him. Before the end of their visit I needed to ask him about the dog.

'What about Bullet?' I asked. 'Won't you take him back home? I feel that I'm imposing on the family who are looking after him.'

'Only on condition that you bring him back yourself,' he replied.

If I was to collect him, it seemed best to arrange this without delay in case I should suddenly go into labour. I asked the sister if I could have permission to leave the hospital, take a bus, and collect the dog to return him. She agreed, but instead of authorizing a trip by bus, she arranged for the social welfare worker, Mrs Jenkins, to take me by car. Mrs Jenkins had already been to see me in hospital and was responsible for coordinating with the other social workers involved in the case. I bought a box of chocolates for the family and put some money in an envelope to cover the cost of the dog food. The next day I collected Bullet and thanked the family. When I took him to the house, Vincent let him in and closed the door quickly without saying a word. Mrs Jenkins then took me straight back to the hospital.

That evening Vincent and Andy visited me again. Vincent again started asking when I would be able to come home. The staff nurse and two of the ward doctors came along to see us. Vincent was very insistent about wanting to have me back home.

'She needs a lot of rest,' said one of the doctors.

'I'll make sure she gets plenty of rest at home,' said Vincent. 'I'll take care of everything. She's better off at home than here spending her time knitting.'

In the end, after a lengthy discussion on the subject of my blood pressure, Vincent conceded that it was best for me to stay in hospital for another couple of days.

That same night, I went into labour. It was three days after I had been admitted. The contractions started at three o'clock in the morning. When I had given birth to Andy, Vincent had been present. On this occasion, I did not want to disturb his sleep, but more to the point I honestly could not cope with the prospect of him being present at the birth. It was also a totally unsuitable place for Andy to be kept waiting. I simply wanted to have the baby in a calm secure environment entirely on my own.

The nurses who delivered the baby were quietly competent. I did not need any medication. All I asked was to have my back rubbed to see me through each contraction. This way I was able to relax between the contractions. The staff nurse who had taken care of me when I was admitted had asked if she could deliver the baby if she was on duty at the time. To my relief, she arrived to start her shift just in time for the actual birth at seven o'clock in the morning.

All these months I had wondered what the little stranger would look like. The nurse placed the baby on me and announced that it was a little girl. At seven pounds and six ounces she was almost the same weight as Andy had been, just one ounce lighter. She had a funny little face with big round cheeks, deep-set eyes, and a beautiful mouth. Her skin looked a shade darker than Andy's, and she had a shock of black hair. Her tiny little finger nails looked perfectly manicured. Her ears and back were coated in soft, furry hair, whereas Andy had been born without any body hair. When she cried, her little voice had a plaintive tone, which prompted in me a strong maternal urge to protect her.

After I had enjoyed a few minutes with her, I asked if I could ring Vincent to break the news. The nurses said I needed to have a few stitches and offered to phone for me. I said I preferred to tell him myself, so I waited till everything had been sorted out and I was ready to go into the main ward.

'It's all over,' I said trying to contain my excitement. 'I've had the baby. It's a girl.'

'Why didn't you let me know sooner so that I could be present at the birth?' he asked.

'Because it all started in the middle of the night and wouldn't have been convenient for you and Andy.'

'Don't you think I should have been the judge of that?' he retorted, displeased. There was an awkward silence, then I told him how cute the baby was.

'She looks a bit like my grandma,' I added flippantly.

'So you've been to bed with your grandma, have you!'

As ridiculous as this was, I began to wonder if he might reject the baby. 'When are you coming to visit?' I asked.

'I don't know. I don't want anyone there waiting for me.'

It was his paranoia again suggesting that there was some kind of trap waiting for him.

When he finally came later that day, I had the baby beside me in bed. Vincent would not look at her directly. Andy showed a curious interest in her straight away, but at the first sign that he might step out of line, Vincent grew angry with him and threatened to take him straight back home. At each visit they never stayed long, and Vincent never brought me anything unless I specifically asked for something. All the other patients had fruit, cards, flowers, gifts, and lots of visitors. I felt conspicuous with my jug of water and my knitting. But I had my precious baby and that was what mattered most. I asked if Vincent would take some dirty laundry home for me. He gave the impression that this was a lot of trouble and insisted on taking it away in my suitcase. The few essentials that I needed I managed to buy in the hospital shop.

Very soon the baby developed jaundice just as Andy had done soon after birth. Wearing just a nappy and a mask to cover her eyes—like miniature goggles—she was placed in an incubator next to my bed. The treatment involved photo-therapy using light bulbs. The effect of the electric light on the baby's skin helped her to fight off the jaundice. This made her look as if she was on display as a perfect specimen of a full-term baby in an illuminated display cabinet. Most of the time she was curled up lying on her front a bit like a rabbit. Other patients and visitors would stop to look at her making admiring comments.

Again, the next time Vincent came to visit he would not look directly at the baby. He did not want to talk about her either. Looking tired and unkempt, as if looking after Andy was wearing him out, he was still visibly disturbed. He told me he had been busy clearing more stuff out of the house, which I understood referred to building debris. Convinced that he was being followed each time he went out, he even claimed that I had got my family to watch over him. When I asked him what he meant, he intimated that I knew perfectly well what he was talking about. As my bed was in an open ward, it was difficult to talk openly. I preferred to talk on the phone, which was kept in an empty side ward. Later, when we spoke on the phone, I asked him how he felt about the baby. 'She has straight black hair and hair on her back, which isn't natural,' he said. I shuddered, finding his reactions grotesque.

'This is our baby you're talking about in this way.'

'She's not my baby,' he said. 'She's an Indian baby.' I found this rejection very upsetting. Sobbing heavily on the phone, I told him that this was his baby and that he had no right to shirk his responsibility as the baby's father. I found that I had more courage to tell him straight on the phone without fear of being threatened, hit, or intimidated. Although he disliked the way I spoke to him, I did feel that he had taken note. I felt that, with time, he would accept the baby as his own.

I kept Mrs Jenkins, the hospital social welfare worker, informed about Vincent's reactions. She did not like the idea of me going back home with the baby and admitted that she felt very worried about us. I tried to assure her that Vincent would not harm the baby. She decided to call a case conference to discuss the situation with the family doctor and the hospital staff. The result of this was that they needed my assurance that I would keep in communication with Mrs Jenkins once I had returned home. I agreed. It was also arranged for the psychiatrist who had made the last home visit before I had been admitted to hospital to write to Vincent to ask him to attend the psychiatric hospital as an outpatient.

The day after my emotional phone conversation with Vincent, he visited me again. I had taken the baby out of the incubator to breastfeed. When I had finished, I asked him to hold her for a moment. I was unsure how he would react, but I simply thrust her into his arms. He held her and looked at her directly this time. I sorted myself out, then took her back into my arms. Gradually he showed that he was getting used to her. I hoped that his ideas of rejection were fading. He began to show concern about her photo-therapy treatment, suspecting that this was simply an excuse to keep us longer in hospital.

In fact the baby's blood test results bordered on a very serious level to the extent that, for a while, it looked as if she might need to have a blood transfusion. Fortunately in the end this proved unnecessary, and after a few more days she started to respond better to the photo-therapy. Of course, I had to get up several times in the night to feed her and also to give her water. It already seemed like years since I had been able to enjoy a deep, undisturbed night's sleep. We still needed to stay a few more days in hospital until the baby's blood tests showed satisfactory results.

One night Vincent rang the sister's office asking to speak to me. They did not mind me using their phone. He told me he had been sorting out some more things, including some jewellery, and asked if I still wanted my wedding ring. I had left it at home for reasons of security.

'Of course I still want my wedding ring!' I exclaimed in protest. I could see mild amusement on Dr Walker's face. Apparently she had already spoken to Vincent when he had phoned asking about my blood pressure before the baby was born. As she explained to him that they needed to perform a check on the baby using one of the machines, he had immediately become suspicious, thinking she was referring to an ultrasound scan. She had then reassured him that it was simply a matter of a routine check on the baby's heartbeat. The staff nurse had also been subjected to his anxious enquiries about the baby's body hair. She had explained to him that this was perfectly normal for babies of various ethnicities, including European babies.

To my horror Vincent informed me one day that he had phoned my mother. He had described the baby to her and asked her if she thought I was the kind of woman who would sleep with another man. I wondered what could have possessed him to do such a thing. Up to now I had managed to keep the disturbing facts of my predicament from my parents, and I knew how it could worry my mother. Even when she had nothing to worry about, she still worried. Now Vincent had probably alarmed her to the point of making her feel ill. I knew that phoning her would involve me in a lot of uncomfortable questions, so I decided to write and explain that, since his return to work, Vincent had felt under a great deal of stress and was suffering with his nerves. This was the kind of terminology she could relate to.

Soon before I was due to be discharged, I had an unexpected visitor. It was the doctor's secretary who had looked after Bullet. She brought gifts for the baby and bags of fruit for me. I was amazed and delighted to see her. What a considerate, generous person she was. Her visit lifted my spirits, and I felt ready to face the next step.

I had already spent almost two weeks in hospital, including the three days before the baby's birth. Now I longed to go home back to Andy and organize our life with the new baby. Vincent showed almost as much suspicion about the baby's jaundice as he had shown about my blood pressure, even though we had been through a similar ordeal when Andy was born.

I was feeling cautiously optimistic. I was looking forward to spending time looking after Andy and enjoying the comforts of home. It was an opportunity to start afresh with Vincent. He had not mentioned any letter about attending an outpatient clinic at the psychiatric hospital. I obviously could not ask him about this since he was unaware that the the arrangement had been made by the team at my hospital. I expected that, with time, he would accept the idea of talking to doctors again and accept some form of treatment. I was convinced that, if I stood by him, he was bound to gain my confidence and trust. It was that romantic notion that love would conquer all.

Chapter 11

An Attempt at a Fresh Start

The first thing that struck me as I walked through the front door into the living room was the dirt and fluff wafting around like tumble weeds. Vincent obviously had not cleaned up while I had been in hospital. The dogs greeted me enthusiastically and showed great curiosity, sniffing for a long time at the strange new smells until they finally understood what the tiny bundle contained. The house had a strange empty feel. First I noticed the missing furniture. Our swivel armchair was no longer there. A small marble-topped table that Vincent had made and the cowhide rug had also disappeared. The room looked bare with just the two sofas and the coffee table. Then I noticed that the shelf for the television set had been painted white. I walked into the kitchen to discover that the extractor hood over the gas hob had been removed. All my storage jars for sugar, flour, and biscuits had gone. The wall-mounted fittings for kitchen roll and foil had been taken down. Also missing, as I discovered later, were a complete set of willow pattern crockery, three copper saucepans, the laundry basket, pegs, jelly moulds, biscuit cutters, casserole dishes, and a complete set of cutlery.

Later I went down to the basement to discover that the bookshelves were empty except for a volume of the complete works of Shakespeare and a small English dictionary. All my teaching materials had been thrown away along with my collection of books, which included expensive foreign-language dictionaries and reference books for my work. Worst of all, my photo album had gone. This had contained irreplaceable pictures of Andy as a baby. My antique sewing machine had been thrown away as well as Vincent's tools. Even the ladder to the loft, now presumably completely empty, had gone. He had also disposed of Andy's pushchair, the ironing board, and our cameras. I looked in the wardrobe in the bedroom to find that all my trousers had gone. I had never had many clothes anyway. Now all I had left was a couple of dresses and a skirt. He had also decided to throw away the new denim jacket and new jeans that he had bought for himself in the summer.

'Why have you thrown so many valuable things away?' I asked.

'You've brought it all on yourself by refusing to sort out things when I asked you to.'

'I don't know what you mean. I wouldn't have chosen to do without any of the things you've thrown away. Especially the photos which would have been of as much value to the children as to ourselves.' He dismissed this, refusing to accept that they would ever show any interest in them.

'Why have you thrown away your tools?'

'You know the reason.'

He was convinced that I had harboured some strange motive which had prompted such an insane act. Some of the tools had scarcely been used. Naturally, I denied any understanding of the motives he intimated to me.

Later he admitted that it had been when someone had phoned and got the wrong number that he had felt prompted to dispose of the items. He had also felt provoked into blocking up the vent in the bathroom after one of our phone conversations while I was in hospital. When I told him how I would miss the things and expressed concern about the cost of replacing them, he said we could buy new stuff of better quality. I imagined the reaction of whosoever had found all our stuff. What a find!

Certain belongings had mysteriously been spared from the massive clearance. I did not dare mention the set of brown dinner plates and the little lamp in the form of a house, which my sister had bought for Andy, in case he should suddenly decide to throw them out as well. Yet I did not feel broken hearted by the losses. Determined to stay positive about coming home, I told myself that, after all, these were only material things. However, it was the fact that Vincent's mind was still so deeply disturbed that affected me. I tried to hang on to my optimism for as long as possible rather than allow this blow to depress me straight away.

For the first day or two Vincent was in a relatively pleasant mood. We cleaned up the house and changed the beds. There were piles of dirty laundry. The nappies were discoloured, as Vincent had mixed them in the wash with nonfast-coloured clothes. We talked about a name for the baby. We both liked the name Sophie, which seemed to suit her, so we settled on this.

Vincent was still cooking the evening meal and was just as fussy as he had been before. He had stopped using any salt. For fear of contamination, he and Andy only consumed canned milk or milk from cartons. He had been throwing away the bottled milk, so I reduced our daily order. I still used bottled milk for myself. He would eat only a certain brand of sliced white bread. I let him choose the supermarket where we did our weekly food shopping. He was convinced that people would be waiting for him if I chose the store. Even so, he still claimed to be watched by certain shop assistants. He refused to let me buy sugar from the supermarket, presumably because the packaging was blue and white. He refused to buy anything on special offer and insisted on certain brands of tinned food.

As I spent more time with Vincent, my optimism was soon eroded. About three days after I had returned home from hospital, the first trouble started. The midwife had called to make sure the baby was all right. I had removed the baby's changing mat from its usual place in the bathroom and taken it downstairs for Sophie to lie on while she was to be examined. After the midwife had left, Vincent flew into a rage, accusing me of indicating that he had done something wrong in the corner of the bathroom by removing and then replacing the changing mat. Underneath the surface in the bathroom where I changed the baby was a complex of pipework. Vincent unscrewed the surface board and looked inside at the pipes. They had all been painted bright red resembling a tangled mass of blood vessels.

'Do you want me to smash the pipes?' he asked angrily. 'Do you want me to smash the boiler as well?'

'No, of course not!' I replied, trying my best to calm him. 'I don't want anything of the kind. I didn't mean to indicate anything by moving the mat.'

I felt all my optimism about us sharing a future together shatter and fall apart. It was like a single blow to a delicate vessel which had been broken many times before and which had been precariously glued together for the last time before its final disintegration.

113

That night Vincent went on at length showering me with accusations that I did not appreciate any of the work he had done on the house, that I had not lifted a finger to help, and that all I could do was sit back and criticise. It was like listening to a cracked record.

'Do you want a divorce?' he asked. Taken aback, I hesitated, wondering how he would react to the truth. My answer slipped out quietly.

'Yes.'

He clenched his fist and moved towards me as if to punch me. I curled up in defence, but he redirected the blow, which landed with full force in the sofa. I felt certain that he would hit me. I sat there trembling as he continued to rant and rave at the sheer audacity of my confession. Then he went promptly downstairs and fetched out our marriage certificate, which he tore up into pieces and threw at me.

'That's what I think of our marriage,' he said. 'I'll go now and I'm taking Andy with me.'

Had I made a terrible mistake by speaking out? Dr Singh had advised me not to be at all provocative, but on this occasion any attempt to give a more diplomatic reply had been overridden by the temptation to tell the blunt truth. I needed to confront Vincent with the fact that there were limits to what I was prepared to endure.

Vincent headed straight upstairs where Andy was peacefully sleeping. He started packing our one and only suitcase, which was very small. I cried bitterly to release my raw emotions. I knew there was nothing I could do to stop him if he walked out, taking Andy. I could only hope that he would come to his senses, but I had no confidence that he had any basis for making rational decisions. I felt feeble and hated myself for my ineptitude. If only I could use some power of persuasion or come up with a startlingly brilliant idea! But I felt absolutely exhausted, and besides, so far I had had precious little influence on Vincent and his fixed ideas. Feeling at a complete loss, I went upstairs to bed.

Andy did not stir in his sleep. Finally Vincent came into the bedroom.

'I'd better wait till morning,' he said. 'I don't want to disturb Andy now.'

For the moment I felt some relief.

By morning Vincent appeared to have calmed down. The whole incident seemed to have blown over. The threat of him leaving with Andy left me feeling uneasy. When he went out for a while, I took the opportunity to ring Mrs Jenkins. I told her that I was okay but felt shaken up by Vincent's aggression and disturbed behaviour. She asked about the children. I told her that they were okay and that the baby was still recovering well from the jaundice. I assured her that Vincent's aggression had not been in any way directed at the children.

'I'm concerned that you might have a nervous breakdown yourself from the strain.'

'Don't worry,' I assured her. 'Before things reach that point I will leave Vincent. It's something I think about more and more, but it will be difficult to organize an escape with the children. There are the pets to consider as well.'

'You must get things into the right order of priorities,' she added. 'The children must come first.'

'I know.'

'Is there anything I can do to help?' she asked. 'I'll let your health visitor know your situation.'

After the midwife's final visit, my health visitor would take over as my only support. I realized that I had to work out an emergency plan in my mind so that I could feel fully prepared to leave if it proved necessary. This would not be easy. The end of November was approaching. The weather was very cold and frosty. We were living on the remains of my maternity benefit, child benefit, and our meagre savings. With the mortgage payments, other bills, the car, and the pets to feed, money would run out in a few months. We still needed to buy things for the house. Vincent showed no concern about this, and he was in no condition to return to work. He showed little interest in looking after Sophie. In any case, I would have no confidence in his ability to look after the children while I worked. The whole situation was a real mess. The prospect of living from hand to mouth would only make matters worse than they already were.

The health visitor called in while Vincent was busy washing the car. He kept popping in for buckets of clean water. The health visitor was a pleasant young woman and did not pry into our problems. I told her I would come to the clinic in a couple of weeks to weigh the baby and have a chat about any concerns.

Vincent grew impatient whenever Sophie cried. He complained about me carrying her round the house in a sling. I found this practical, as I had both hands free and it helped her to go to sleep easily. He claimed that she would become too dependent on me, but I disagreed without turning the issue into an argument. Andy responded well to the baby. He was still sleeping in a cot, so we needed to buy him a new bed so that the baby could soon sleep there. I ordered a single divan with drawers underneath, useful for storage space. I left a deposit and arranged delivery the following day. Vincent expressed suspicion, saying I had been in too great a hurry. He had expected to be consulted. I told him to go and look at the bed and cancel the order if he was unhappy with my choice. He said it was too late now.

The bed was delivered, and Vincent carefully removed the labels from the bed base. He complained about the quality of the bed and also about an unpleasant remark that he claimed one of the delivery men had made. He had interpreted the man's remark about the dogs as a personal insult, which made no sense to me.

We also needed new curtains for our bedroom. Vincent went to buy these, but he had not made allowance for shrinkage in the wash and they were already much too short. Vincent preferred to think that someone had come into the house and changed them. I went to buy a longer pair and decided to use the old curtains to make cushion covers for the dogs' beds. Vincent had thrown away the other cushion covers I had made. Without a sewing machine it would take a long time to make these, so I planned to return to the craft classes after Christmas and looked forward to taking Andy and the baby.

One afternoon Vincent took Andy out to buy a new coat for him. After spending the whole afternoon looking round the shops, he settled on a brown duffel coat, which looked lovely on him. The next day I went to hang up the coat and noticed that Vincent had removed the loop, all the labels inside the coat, and a complete set of toggles on one side. Each time he bought something new, Vincent felt compelled to check it over and remove all the labels. Another day he took Andy to buy a new bike, which was to be an early Christmas present. He taught him to ride it, and before long our son was whizzing round the living room on it. It was lovely to see him enjoy his new gift.

Sometimes tensions mounted when I grew impatient about the times when Vincent took over futile preoccupations, but it was his increasing aggression that really drove me to my wit's end. One night there were three things, one after the other, that caused him grief. First Andy decided to help me draw the curtains, and as he tugged, the curtain rail fell down. I told Vincent not to get involved. I would fix it. But he accused me of pulling the rail down myself as a way of communicating to the neighbours. Next he discovered that we had no onions. He had decided to make meatballs for dinner and refused to accept that I had simply forgotten to buy onions. Third was the ultimate annoyance, which would have been hilariously funny had he not taken the matter so deadly seriously. With the intention of rolling the meatballs in flour, he lifted a big jar from the kitchen shelf, which he had reorganized, tipped some of the contents onto a plate, and rolled the meatballs—all before I had the chance to tell him that it was, in fact, icing sugar, not flour. Absolutely furious at this, he grabbed a long sharp kitchen knife and held it to my face while he lectured me. I thought he was going to kill me. I dared not flinch. Inside I was petrified.

Again it took me a while to recover from shaking and to come to terms with what had just happened. I wondered in what ways this stress was taking its toll on my own health. Even if I could deal with the stress, this was not the way I chose to live my life. Furthermore, I simply could not allow the children to be exposed to this constant unpredictable aggression.

Before I had the chance to regain my composure, another outburst occurred which eclipsed everything and precipitated my final decision to leave. Without any provocation whatsoever, Vincent stormed into the kitchen from the basement where he had been doing some work in sand and cement. He flew into a rage and struck the worktop with his trowel. He continued to chop at the edge of the worktop releasing his wild fury while Andy and I stood back motionless to avoid the flying debris. When he finally stopped, there was a deep gash left in the worktop with sharp jagged edges. Somehow an association struck me between the gaping wound in the worktop and the anguish that his violence was inflicting on me, whether directly or indirectly. There were splashes of grey sand

and cement all over the curtains and the ceiling. It was as if his brain had exploded releasing splatters of grey matter. I was again reduced to a trembling wreck, horrified at the display of destruction, this time witnessed by Andy. I had no idea what had prompted this outburst, but I had now reached the tipping point.

Mindful of the predictions by Dr Walker, that my homecoming could prompt a turning point in Vincent's behaviour, it was abundantly clear that no improvement was in sight. I now decided once and for all that I could not stay. I simply had to find a way to leave with the children. I could tolerate no more. It was simply too unsafe.

Chapter 12

Woeful Friday

Having reached my decision, I now had to figure out how I could actually leave with both children. If Vincent went out, which was not at all often, it was unannounced. The only time I went out with both Andy and Sophie was when I took the dogs for a walk. On the few occasions when I needed to leave Sophie with Vincent for a short while, he complained about her crying and quickly lost patience. On one occasion he instructed me never to leave him with her again, otherwise he would throw her through the window. Though I did not believe he would ever do such a thing, I decided it was obviously best to avoid the possibility that any bad situation might arise. After that I would place Sophie at one end of the pram and sit Andy at the other until we reached the park.

Vincent needed a lot of sleep and always got up late, so it seemed that the best plan would be to leave early in the morning. I usually got up to feed the baby in the early hours and again at about six o'clock. After his violent reaction to my interest in divorce and his intention to keep Andy, I realized that there was no way that I could tell him that we were leaving. If I could be criticized for this deception, so be it. For a couple of nights I lay awake trying to get used to the prospect of homelessness. Foremost in my mind was the urgency of being in danger at home. If anything should happen to me, the children would be seriously at risk. I cried silent tears for hours each night in bed and lived on nervous energy by day.

A month after my homecoming, on a Friday, which fell two weeks before Christmas, Andy woke early and we got up without disturbing

Vincent. Overnight there had been a hard frost. After I fed Sophie, as soon as we were dressed and had had a hot drink, I went to the basement and took all the documents I thought we might need. In case Vincent woke up, I had decided not to take any other belongings, except for the car. After all, our need was greater than his. It had occurred to me that the sound of the front door closing might disturb his sleep. If he heard us and followed us, at least with the car I could be sure of a quick getaway. I hastily scraped the frost off the windows. As well as a cold, Andy had a slight infection in his toe and could not walk far.

I headed straight for the social services office. I felt uneasy waiting in the reception area in case Vincent should suddenly appear. Then Charles appeared, the social worker who had successfully persuaded Vincent to be admitted to hospital. I refreshed his memory in case he was unable to place me. I explained that we had just left home. He told me that the social worker in charge of our case was not at work that Friday so he offered to give us a lift to the Homeless Families Unit, which was a short distance away. Although I had our car, I accepted the lift, as I wanted to talk to him. He felt that I had done the right thing to leave home. I gave him some examples of Vincent's recent behaviour, which had forced my decision.

'Vincent really ought to be in hospital,' he said. 'I'm sorry things worked out badly for you after his admission and swift discharge.'

'He has begged me not to try to help him get treatment,' I said. 'Even though I obviously disagree with him, it's his choice to remain as he is.'

'Do you have any money?' he asked.

'Yes, enough for a few days. Thank you for your help.'

At the Homeless Families Unit we had a long wait. It was already crowded with people waiting, and everyone looked really depressed. Finally I was interviewed and then went to the shop to buy some essentials for the day. My bones moaned with the cold. For a while we walked along behind a policeman in the street, feeling reassured in case Vincent should suddenly appear. I put the shopping in the car and parked in a side street. After another long wait, the assistant told me that there was a place for us in a unit with bedding and cooking equipment about three miles away. She still needed to check that the unit still had everything that we would need. This involved another long wait. There was a public phone in the hallway. As I had not left a note for Vincent, I began to feel I ought to call him, intending to keep the conversation brief.

'Hello. It's me, Nicki.'

'Hello.'

'Well, we've left home.'

'Why did you take the car? I need it. It belongs to me.'

'You can have it back when I'm ready. At the moment I need it more than you.'

'Why did you take Andy?'

I hastily said goodbye and put down the phone. His first concern was about the car! He sounded really angry, as I had expected. Nevertheless I felt upset and struggled to hold back the tears.

Eventually the assistant told me the address of the unit, but said that the caretaker would not be there till five o'clock. As it was now only two o'clock, we drove off to stop for something to eat on the way. The baby slept nearly all day, completely oblivious to the upheaval facing us. I kept her in the sling the whole time to keep her warm. For a while, to keep out of the cold, we walked round a store. Andy was content to watch programmes on the television sets on display. I bought him a small Lego set to play with. It was depressing having nowhere to go all afternoon on such a cold day. I was wearing my new winter shoes, but my legs were bare. Though I had no socks or tights, it did not occur to me to buy any. My mind was on other things.

Finally we went round to the building where the unit was housed. The caretaker showed us to our room on the first floor. It was gloomy and cold. There was a washbasin, a gas cooker, but no cooking equipment. The bed had only one blanket, and there was a cot. There was a small electric fire and a table and two chairs. I briefly explained our situation, saying I had been led to understand that we would be provided with more than this. He said we should go home the next day to fetch more belongings. As the next day was a Saturday, there would be no one at the social services office to help me out. I therefore had no option but to ask for a police escort. The caretaker said that he would check on us the next day to make sure that everything was okay.

That night I did not sleep at all. We huddled together wearing all our clothes in bed with the blanket over us. I shivered all night long. I was also restless wondering what I needed to collect from the house and concerned about having to confront Vincent so soon. In the night I had little idea of the time, having neither a watch nor a clock. When it was daylight, I got up feeling stale. We now had toothpaste and toothbrushes but no towel. Somehow we managed.

Periodically I would be overwhelmed by a wave of extreme fatigue that plunged me into a state in which I felt that I could barely keep my head above water. After I had been deprived of sleep for so many nights, there was little prospect of respite from the relentless demands on my increasingly frail physical and emotional resources.

There had been another heavy frost overnight so it took a while to clear the car windows. It must have been about nine thirty when we reached the local police station. I explained my predicament to the desk officer.

'Why have you brought the children with you?'

'Because there's absolutely no one I can leave them with.' I was made to feel as though I was causing them a great deal of inconvenience.

'Go to your house. A police car will be there by the time you arrive.'

I parked the car across the road from the house and gave Andy a chocolate bar to eat while I went up to the waiting police car. I had the baby in the sling. There were two policemen, one in uniform and the other in plain clothes. I explained my problem to them through the car window.

'What is it about your husband's behaviour that makes you think he's mentally ill?' one of them asked. I gave a few examples, explaining that he had been admitted to hospital but had discharged himself before receiving treatment. They agreed to escort me on condition that I collected only basic essentials. They rang the doorbell and asked me to stay in the background while they spoke to Vincent. He was dressed and let us in. When the officer asked if I might collect some belongings, Vincent appeared to be surprised that this was all I had come for, saying that a police escort was unnecessary. He started to ask me why I had left home.

'This is not the time to discuss my reasons,' I replied. 'Let's not hold up the police any longer than necessary.' Vincent became more insistent, and the policemen suggested we contact our solicitors over the matter.

I started to make my way upstairs to collect some bedding. Vincent had put all Andy's toys together in his bedroom. I took the new duvet from Andy's bed and a blanket. We had just spent over £100 on bedding for

Andy's new bed. Vincent came upstairs to me. For a moment I thought he was going to hit me. He looked so angry.

'Don't leave, Nicki. Don't do it. Don't do it.'

'I have no choice. I don't want to but I have to.'

We were both speaking loudly enough for the policemen to hear us. Vincent continued to implore me to stay.

'Then why do you keep threatening to kill me in the way that you do?' I asked feeling agitated.

'It's not what I'll do to you that you need to worry about now,' he said. 'It's what I'll do to myself.'

I understood by this that he was referring to a suicide attempt. I had not been prepared for this. I was determined not to weaken or feel sorry for him. I dragged the bedclothes down the stairs and headed straight for the car. Vincent followed me. He overtook me and reached the car just before I did. Andy was sitting on the back seat. The policemen kept well out of the way staying inside the house. Vincent climbed into the driver's seat pushing me aside, but I held on to the door and put my arm inside it to prevent him from closing it. He still tried to close the door, even with my arm trapped inside it taking the blows. All this time I still had Sophie in the sling. As I pulled my arm free, I still clutched at the door, panic stricken at the thought of Vincent taking Andy away from me. Finally I caught my fingers as Vincent slammed the door shut. Two women at the bus stop started to call out. I told one of them to fetch the police out of the house. They came quickly as Vincent started the engine and tried to manoeuvre the car out of the parking space. As the driver of a big van blocked his exit, Vincent mounted the car on to the pavement in an effort to escape that way, but there were too many obstacles. A small crowd had gathered to watch the commotion. Suddenly realising that I had my car keys, I suggested to the police that, by opening the tailgate, we could get Andy out of the car.

'Have you forgotten that you've got a baby round your neck?' said the policeman. 'Don't stir up trouble!'

I stood there in a daze, shocked at the policeman's accusations and unable to believe how horribly wrong things were turning out. The officer in uniform spoke gently to Vincent through the car window, addressing him by his first name and asking him politely to come into the house to talk things over. Realizing that there was no way he could escape, Vincent lifted Andy out of the car and held him firmly in his arms. The policemen had called for more help, and a police van appeared but stayed in the background. Eventually Vincent agreed and carried Andy into the house. The women at the bus stop came up to me and tried to reassure me.

'He's very ill' was all I could say in Vincent's defence. I picked up the bedclothes and put them in the back of the car. I waited anxiously. After a few minutes, a senior policeman came over to speak to me. 'We're not in a position to act on your behalf and take your son from your husband. It's not a criminal matter but a domestic one.'

'No, you're wrong,' I corrected him. 'It's a medical matter. My husband has a serious mental illness, and I'm afraid he may not be capable of looking after our son.'

'In that case you must contact a solicitor immediately. There are some excellent solicitors who will be able to act without delay and enforce an emergency order. Vincent intends to claim custody of both your children.'

I felt totally shocked by this. Never before had Vincent expressed the slightest interest in claiming Sophie in the event of a separation.

'With regard to the car, your husband tells us he has contacted the insurance company and had your name withdrawn from the policy. I don't know if this is true, but you seem to have enough problems to contend with as it is. We'll give you a lift in the van when you're ready. But first your husband wants to have a word with you again.'

I went back into the house feeling outsmarted, humiliated, and downhearted. Andy was on the sofa looking bewildered but glad to be home.

'Look,' said Vincent. 'We can sort this out. Don't contact a solicitor before we've talked things over. We can sort this all out without a solicitor.'

'No, we can't sort this out ourselves,' I insisted. 'That's just the point. You keep refusing to see a doctor or speak to anyone at all about your problems.'

'All right,' said Vincent. 'If you want me to get my head shrunk . . . '

'It's not a matter of getting your head shrunk. All you have to do is agree to talk to somebody who can help you.' I refused to discuss the matter any further, feeling deeply distressed that he had taken Andy. I agreed to ring him later on.

On the way back to our accommodation, the plainclothes officer advised me not to give Vincent my address or phone number. By this time I was drowning in my tears.

'I'm in a terrible trap,' I sobbed. 'First he threatens to kill me. Now he threatens to kill himself.'

Again the baby slept through the whole drama. The neighbours must have been burning with curiosity. The van that had blocked the car's exit had caused quite a queue of traffic, so the incident attracted a lot of attention. The car was left parked half on the pavement at an angle. I expected Vincent to be furious with me for involving him in such a public scene. Yet, in the presence of the police, he had been all calm and collected. Not for the first time, I was the one who appeared to be the hysterical one.

Back in the dismal bed-sitting room I cried another river. I felt like a terrible failure and an outcast. How could the police be so unsympathetic? My bruised arm and fingers felt very tender but did not feel as battered as my self-esteem, which had now reached an all-time low.

I realized I still needed to go to the shops before they closed. All I had managed to take from home was a duvet and a blanket. As I went into a store to buy a towel, a mug, and some cutlery, I was still on the verge of tears all the time. As if to heighten my misfortunes, the shops were decorated with colourful festive displays and bustling with Christmas shoppers. By the time I reached the checkout to pay, I had tears streaming down my face again, adding to my embarrassment. It was simply impossible to stem the tide.

I rushed back down the road to the house. The caretaker arrived and I explained what had happened when I had gone home to collect belongings. He had children himself and helped me to try to understand what it must have felt like for Vincent after we had left him. He could not stay long. I was desperate to talk to someone. As he left, the woman in the room above mine came down and asked what the matter was. I sat upstairs with Sharon for a long time talking and felt much better as a result. She took a real interest in the baby, which also cheered me up. As I told her about my situation, she made pertinent remarks, which I found myself taking very seriously. 'You love him very much, don't you?' she said, in just the same way as Dr Singh had said. Inevitably, each time I heard people say this made me feel even more emotional.

'From what you tell me, you strike me as representing the opposite of Vincent.'

'It's never mattered to me that we're so different. What matters far more is our interests and our aims and the fact that we enjoy each other's company.'

I decided it was time to phone Vincent. I was still in a highly charged emotional state.

'Come home,' he said. 'Why put yourself through all this misery and discomfort?'

'I want to come home. I really do. But I need time to think things over.'

'What is there to think about?' he asked. 'Just tell me where you are and I'll come and fetch you now.'

'I need more time. Besides, you'll never forgive me for leaving you and everything that's happened.'

'Nicki, I will. Of course, I'll forgive you. I love you. Everything I've done the past few years has been for you. For you and the children. Why ruin all that?'

It had been a long time since I had heard him express any affection in this way. The conversation continued briefly without me feeling able to submit completely. Vincent wanted me to go home straight away, afraid that any delay and careful reflection might make me change my mind. He tried to make it sound as if I had only one chance. If I refused now, I might not have another chance.

'I'll spend one more night here just to give myself more time to think' was my final response.

He sounded so warm and loving that I realized I could too easily overlook the horrors I had been through with him. I went back up to Sharon's room to tell her the gist of the conversation. She offered me a meal, but I could not eat. I felt very impressionable, but the decision had to be mine and mine alone. It was no use relying on other people's opinions and advice. The relief I felt in talking about my problems gave me the strength to clarify my thoughts and face the problems afresh. I had been deprived of so much sleep and been on such an emotional roller coaster ride—it had all driven me to the point of distraction.

On reflection, I realized just how disastrous the day had been. It had been badly planned. I should not have taken the car. I should have stood up to the police more assertively. When I had gone home, I should have kept Andy and the baby well out of the way by enlisting the help of social services, thus avoiding running into a weekend. Fridays proved to be highly problematic. Now Andy had witnessed another traumatic scene.

I should have negotiated terms and conditions with Vincent if I was to concede to his wish for us to return home. I wondered if Vincent had been sincere when he had said that he was prepared to consider seeing a psychiatric professional. Maybe this short separation was sufficient at least to get him to agree to seek help. Somehow I found myself repeating over and over in my head the marriage vow, 'in sickness and in health'. I still cared for Vincent enough to be persuaded to give him one last chance. How had it happened that I had been so badly derailed from the ultimate aim to achieve psychiatric help for him?

The bottom line was that Vincent had taken Andy. This presented me with only one choice. The next morning I phoned for Vincent to come and fetch us home.

Chapter 13

Facing Facts

Although I had only been away for two days, it felt more like a whole week. I had caught a heavy cold and felt completely worn out. That evening Vincent cooked a lovely meal for us and he offered to get up the next morning with Andy so that I could have a lie-in. Before going to sleep we talked for a long time about what had happened. I felt relieved that Vincent was not angry with me for the scene outside the house. For once he saw the humorous side of it and said we had put on a good show for the neighbours. He never failed to surprise me with his responses!

When the policemen had been talking with him in the living room, Vincent claimed that one of the officers kept looking up at the ceiling. Vincent had the impression that he had made a mistake in the pattern in the plasterwork. In his usual paranoid way he felt that he was indicating something to him. I tried to reassure him that there was no significance to be read into this. Vincent also had the impression that the reason I had left home had something to do with the work he had been doing the day before. What he was referring to was an incident that had in fact been a really close shave. Andy had got in the way when a door had almost fallen on him. Vincent had taken it off its hinges while he fitted some carpet. It was a carpet remnant which he was fitting in the front entrance. He had hesitated over the correct way to do the work, had consulted me several times, and had finally lost his temper. I had decided at the time never again to ask Vincent to do any work in the house. It had been my idea to use the carpet remnant left over from the new stair carpet. As a result Vincent had immediately suspected me of engineering the incident.

'We left out of a genuine concern for our safety,' I explained, but he could neither understand nor accept that our safety was at risk because of him. 'If you ever hurt me again or carry out these frequent threats to put me in hospital, the children's security would be seriously compromised.'

'Look, Nicki. I'd sooner smash something up than hurt you.'

'Then why the constant threats?' I asked.

'I feel as though it's my only weapon,' he replied. Yet he took not the slightest notice of the bruises on my arm and fingers from my attempt to stop him closing the car door. Previously he had never shown an ounce of remorse or any interest in my injuries from his attacks. He seemed totally incapable of realizing how much he could hurt me either mentally or physically.

I asked him how he had spent his time while we had been away. He had bought himself a new jacket, trousers, and shoes. On the first evening he told me that he had been out with a friend from years back. They had gone out for a drink and come home late. He had told this friend that I had left home, but had not given away any details. He was still not prepared to take anyone into his confidence. He had also decided to join a dance class as a way of making an effort to go out and mix with people. This seemed out of character and amused me slightly, though I did not dare show my amusement. I felt glad that he had decided to mix socially, yet it puzzled me that he should only decide to do this after I had left him. How could he suddenly overcome his acute paranoia in order to go out like this? If he did continue to attend the dance classes as he intended, I would be able to enjoy some time to myself at home. Of course, he did not continue to attend.

The next morning when I was due for my lie-in, the doorbell rang. Vincent went to see who it was. Andy had already climbed into our bed, and Sophie had gone back to sleep after her early-morning feed. After closing the front door, Vincent stormed upstairs, threw a parcel at me, and ripped the television cable out of the socket, smashing the TV set to pieces on the floor. Andy and I looked on in horror and amazement. He then rushed into the bathroom and kicked in the cupboard doors under the washbasin, leaving a mess all over the floor. I sat in bed trembling at the sound of this trail of destruction. Returning to the bedroom, he tore open my parcel. It was simply a Christmas present from my mother—some clothes for Andy and Sophie. How could Vincent be angry over this? He ordered me, in no uncertain terms, to contact my family and instruct them never to send anything to the house. Neither were they to write or to phone.

I got out of bed and started clearing up the mess. The TV had made a deep dent in the floor, which Vincent later patched up, still in a fuming temper. He refused to do anything about the cupboard doors in the bathroom, so I repaired them myself a few days later when I found the time.

When he had calmed down, I asked him why he had been so angry. He said it was something about the way the postman had handed to parcel over to him, which he had interpreted as a gesture of abuse. As for my family, I phoned first my mother then my sister while Vincent was out. I told them Vincent was still suffering from a nervous breakdown. I did not dare give more details than that. I kept telling myself that, once his condition began to improve, I would be able to tell them more. This acute phase of his illness had now been going on for six months. I still convinced myself that, at some point, he would start to emerge from this phase and begin to show signs of recovery. I continued to clutch at my optimism while suspecting that in reality true recovery was nigh on impossible.

My sister took the news very badly. When I asked her not contact me, she had the impression that it was I who had decided I didn't want any contact. I tried to reassure her, but realized that it would be impossible for her and my parents to understand. I could not reveal the truth of what was happening, as it was too horrific. They knew nothing about my attempt to leave home, the seriousness of Vincent's illness, the violent outbursts, and the repercussions on me.

A couple of days later, Vincent decided to throw away my old goat fur lined coat, which, after years of dog walking and accumulated dirt, was in a very sorry state. No wonder I had not been taken seriously by the police and others. I must have looked a complete wreck as well as feeling like one. We went together to buy a new coat. On the way Vincent decided to call in at the police station. Apparently, when I had left home taking the car, he had tried to have me prosecuted for theft of the car! He had decided to go ahead with the charge to serve as an example to me. I found this too ridiculous to take seriously. He took Andy with him while I waited in the car with Sophie. When he returned, he said the police would not take up the charge after all. They must have thought it was an oddball idea for him to charge his wife with taking the family car, even though it was registered in his name.

This time I was the one being indecisive. I could not choose between two coats. They were both green and inexpensive. Vincent suggested I should take both, so for once I afforded myself this extravagance. This way I could have a wash and a wear, much more practical than canvas lined with goat fur when it came to dog paw marks, sticky little fingers, and baby dribble. Then we spent a long time looking for new shoes for Andy, as Vincent was so particular about everything we bought. Once we got back home, he again took great pains to remove all the labels.

One evening he went through the entire record and audio cassette collection removing hand-written notes and all the cards inside the cassette cases. His paranoia was also just as strong. One day he puzzled over a footprint in a pile of sand in the garden claiming that someone must have climbed over the fence into the garden. He refused to entertain the probability that it was, in fact, his own footprint. After fitting two new bolts on the front door of the basement, he jammed them shut so tight that I could not open them. He changed the lock on the main front door and erased the serial numbers on the keys, utterly convinced that someone was coming into the house. Whenever I spoke on the phone, he became suspicious that I was relaying secret messages about him.

One evening we were watching an interesting TV documentary about stress. There were interviews with various people who talked openly about their problems with work and personal relationships. Many of them found great relief by joining support groups. While we were watching, I asked Vincent if he would be willing to attend a group session of this kind. I expected him to reject the suggestion outright, but to my surprise, he said he would be quite willing to go along to one and listen in. This was surely some kind of breakthrough. We had stumbled on the programme completely by chance, so there was no reason for him to raise suspicions, not that he needed any reason. I felt really pleased. Could this prove to be a new cause for hope?

After watching another programme in what turned out to be a series, I sent off for some information, which took a few weeks to arrive. This consisted of an article on depression, which I found very interesting. It was the first literature I had come across on the subject of mental illness. It also included a long list of centres for counselling, which was to prove to be extremely useful. We took our time and looked through the list of centres. Some of them specialised in sexual problems or religion. I picked one at random which appeared to be of a general nature. It was situated in Central London. Vincent approved of the choice, and a couple of days later he phoned up for an initial appointment. As it was almost Christmas, he had to wait until mid-January for the first appointment.

The wait for the date to come round seemed intolerable as Vincent's aggression, paranoia, and obsessive behaviour continued without any signs of improvement. I found some measure of relief in my visits to the health clinic. I did not attend regularly and did not reveal much about Vincent at first, but I had given Mrs Jenkins my assurance that I would keep in touch in this way. It certainly had a therapeutic effect on me to talk a little about the home situation. When the health visitor asked if there was any practical way she could be of help, I asked her to tell me everything she knew about schizophrenia. I was hungry for more factual information and asked if she could send off for some literature from the National Schizophrenia Fellowship, which had been mentioned on one of the TV programmes. I could not risk receiving this through the post at home, as Vincent would not tolerate the very mention of the term *schizophrenia*.

In the meantime, my postnatal check-up was due. Because of Vincent's hostile feelings towards Dr Singh, I had arranged to have my check-up at the hospital. Vincent drove me there, and I went in to ask how long it would take. As it was likely to involve a long wait, I asked Vincent to go home with Andy, and as soon as I was ready, I would phone for him to collect me. The sister who worked with Dr Wardle during my antenatal visits saw me straight away and asked how I was and how Vincent was. I brought her up to speed and explained how anxious I was to find out more about his illness. She was very concerned for me and said she would try to contact Dr Green, the psychiatrist at the hospital where Vincent had been admitted. I could hardly believe it when she told me that Dr Green was on her way over to talk to me. I just had time after my check-up to feed and change the baby when Dr Green appeared.

She told me the staggering statistics—about one person in every hundred in the developed world was diagnosed at some stage of his or her lifetime with schizophrenia. She went on to explain that it was caused by a bio-chemical impairment, which could be treated with medication. For most patients, this proved to be effective with few side effects. However, there was no cure. As for the root cause, it was understood to be largely genetic, though more research was needed. Drug abuse could also act as a trigger. Left untreated, the illness would follow a course of relapses and worsen with age.

This was a lot for me to take in. I told the doctor about my new hopes through the counselling service. When I told her the name of the counselling centre, she said she had heard of it and that it was highly recommended. She offered to contact the centre to acquaint them with Vincent's case once a course of appointments had been arranged for him. I thanked her for her help and arranged to phone her eventually from home to let her know the name of Vincent's counsellor.

At long last it appeared that I had genuine reason to feel optimistic. As I lay awake in bed that night, I went over in my mind the points I had learned about schizophrenia in order to digest all the implications. At least now I knew that there was a good chance that, with the correct medication, we might be able to stay together as a family and get our lives back on track. It was a blow to be told that there was no cure. I had assumed all along that, at some point in the future, Vincent would turn back into the man I had married. After six months of living with Vincent during this acute stage of his illness with no sign of improvement, I needed to face up to the prospect that he would never regain his previous amicable nature.

I began to wonder if there might have been a history of mental illness in Vincent's family. But I would never know if this was the case. Coming from a well-educated family, his father had worked as an electrician. After graduating at a Scottish university, Vincent's paternal grandfather had married a Scottish woman and returned with her to live in Jamaica. Vincent remembered only once visiting his Scottish grandmother during his early childhood. He said that his relatives did not talk about his grandfather and that he did not know the reason for this or know what had happened to them.

The incidence of the schizophrenia was incredibly high at one person in a hundred in the developed world. Perhaps it could be argued that, by going back far enough to examine the past history, most families might include sufferers. The hereditary factor implied that some families would have a higher concentration than others. I also wondered if Vincent's previous cannabis smoking habit might have played a part in triggering his psychosis. The worst fear, almost too unbearable to contemplate, was the implication that our children may have inherited a genetic disposition to develop the illness.

It was several more weeks before I received the information from the National Schizophrenia Fellowship. I kept it hidden in my sewing bag. The information reinforced everything that Dr Green had told me. I learned more about the different types of schizophrenia, the medication, the corresponding ages when symptoms begin to manifest, and the utmost importance of the family in providing care for the patient. It was this emphasis on the critical element of family support that reinforced my decision that I could not leave Vincent. There was no one else who cared about him.

After his initial interview at the counselling centre, Vincent was asked to attend an appointment with the resident psychiatrist. Meanwhile, the interviewer had asked him to register with a new family doctor, as he had adamantly refused to do this. The process of registering with a new GP took several weeks. The slightest pressure from me would have put at risk any progress we might have made. Vincent finally decided on a group practice that had been recommended to me by someone called Val, who had talked to me at the playgroup. She had recently changed her GP herself.

I started to take Andy and Sophie to the playgroup again at the beginning of the new term in January. As before, I always looked forward to chatting to the other mothers, and Andy enjoyed the assortment of toys and activities. He was still quite sensitive and would never wander far away from me to play. I found it reassuring to hear other mothers also express concern about aspects of their children's behaviour. At two months old,

Sophie received a lot of attention and enjoyed watching the children play. At the Wednesday morning craft classes where I used the sewing machine, I met up again with Chris from the flat across the road. As well as coming across Chris in the park when she was walking her dog, I now used to bump into Val from the playgroup. Val also had a son the same age as Andy and a dog, a large, fluffy Alsatian. How I enjoyed their company! The chance meetings in the park and the regular contact at the playgroup lifted my spirits enormously and helped me feel much less isolated.

When Chris heard that I did not have a sewing machine at home, she invited me to come and use hers at her flat. It was taking me ages to finish making the cushion covers for the dogs' beds, which was a simple enough task. Besides, she had invited me over several months ago for a cup of tea, and I had always given a heap of excuses knowing that I'd still be unable to return the invitation. I wanted to tell her what was on my mind, but did not know her well enough. When she asked if Vincent was unemployed, I told her that he had taken some sick leave and now wanted to finish the work on the house before starting a new job.

This was now true, as Vincent had received a letter from his previous employer notifying him of the termination of his employment due to prolonged absence. At last Vincent agreed to apply for benefits using medical certificates from his new GP, which simply stated that he was suffering from depression. In addition to the money we had spent on living expenses, furniture, a stair carpet, bedclothes, and other household essentials, we had also bought tools and clothes to replace those that Vincent had recklessly thrown away. Vincent still smoked heavily and insisted on good quality food. Materials for the work on the house also involved further expense.

After taking a break from working on the front of the house, Vincent had completed the work to the outside toilet but instructed me never to go in there. Next he started making plans for the garden so that Andy would be able to play outside. He was concerned about the steps leading down from the backyard into the basement, which were steep. The sheer drop beside the steps also posed a potential danger.

There were two main considerations that bothered me about the idea of Vincent doing further work of this kind. One was the possibility that any more violent outbursts might prompt me to take the children and leave home for good. The other consideration was the prospect that he would exhaust himself again and feel exasperated by his confusion. Yet the alternative of having him moping around the house with nothing much to occupy his time would also be intolerable. In spite of his frequent accusations that I failed to appreciate his efforts, he did gain satisfaction from completing this work. I therefore decided to support his plans, but only on condition that this was his own undertaking and that he needed to pace himself without getting exhausted, not that I had ever previously put pressure on him. On the contrary, I had always shown concern about the long hours that he worked on the house.

The first complication was the work needed to change the steps. He discussed the detailed plans with me and took his time putting the plans into action. We decided on a low wall along the edge of the yard and shallow steps to make it safer. Each evening for a week he talked about the different ways the work could be done, and asked me for my opinion. He seemed to need guidance at every stage of the planning.

Reluctantly he took a break from the work to attend his counselling appointments each Wednesday at five o'clock. Much to his annoyance, he also had a number of appointments with the welfare office to sort out the confusion over the start date of his benefits claims. Then there were appointments with the new GP, a female doctor, who helped him feel at ease when they talked. I was careful not to press him to disclose any details about their conversations. In his own time he told me that he had talked to her a little about the work he was doing and that the rest was a general chat.

One evening while Vincent was out, I phoned Dr Green to follow up as we had agreed. She explained that, as far as the counselling was concerned, she was unable to intervene after all due to procedures concerning confidentiality. It would be up to the counsellors themselves to ask for information from medical sources if they thought it necessary.

'What can I do if Vincent is violent towards me again?' I asked.

'You'll have to call the police,' she replied. 'They can have him forcibly admitted if necessary. This may be the only way in the end.'

'How serious would this have to be to merit an admission of this kind?'

'If you feel afraid, that's quite serious enough.'

To my mind, on a logistical level, this was highly problematic. I had already experienced fear and explained my experiences to other medical staff on many occasions. To Dr Green it seemed to be clear cut. According to Dr King, as well as one of the senior consultants and the police, who had all reached the same conclusion that our trouble amounted to nothing more than a marital dispute, I was the one alleged to have stirred up trouble. To Dr Singh, the other senior consultant, the social workers, and the hospital staff from the maternity unit, there was no doubt that Vincent ought to be in hospital.

Vincent's lack of insight into his own condition resulted directly in his rejection of medical help. He constructed all manner of paranoid reasons to explain away his feelings. According to Vincent himself, there was nothing much wrong with him other than mild depression and irritability. At home with a small baby and a two-year-old, trying my best to get help and support, it felt very much like a hit-and-miss affair. Was I fooling myself that some progress had been made, that it was just a matter of time before medication would be prescribed? Better to cling to optimism than wallow in despair, I thought. I was left with no alternative but to wait and see what would happen next.

Chapter 14

Faltering Progress

The weeks went by. At about five months, Sophie was old enough to be placed in the bouncer. This consisted of a long thick vertical elastic band attached to a hook in the ceiling beam at one end and to a seat which, when adjusted to the baby's height, enabled the baby's feet to touch the floor. With the music playing and the dogs and cat cruising around her, Sophie would dangle from the beam, push herself with one foot on the floor, and bounce up and down stroking the pets as they brushed by her. Andy had enjoyed the bouncer too at the same age. He now liked to walk around carrying his toy rabbit in the baby sling, which I fastened round his back firmly by doubling up the straps to remove the slack. The rabbit's ears would flop about making it look like a very cute baby.

The frequency of Vincent's appointments with the counselling centre psychiatrist had changed from weekly to fortnightly and, finally, to once a month. I wondered why it was taking such a long time for him to be prescribed appropriate medication. With each appointment I thought to myself that surely this time he would come home with some tablets. In the meantime, his aggressive outbursts continued much as before.

One evening after dinner I remarked that it was taking a long time to get back to normal. How insensitive of me! Vincent interrogated me, holding a knife to my face. 'What do you mean, normal? I've told you, things will never be as they were before. The past is finished. It can only be different now. Why can't you ever be satisfied?'

He went on at length with mounting aggression which culminated in him tearing the arm off his stereo turntable deck, bending it, and throwing it on to the floor.

On another evening, after I had spent all afternoon preparing a roast dinner, he showed his anger at something I considered to be trivial by emptying the freshly prepared food from the plates and dishes all over the floor then ordering me to clean it all up. In the end he helped to do it, but only after I broke down in tears.

'I love you.' I pleaded. 'I want to help you stop these outbursts, but I find it impossible. Please help me to help you.' He did not respond.

Then, sometime after this incident, he started discussing a gap in the garden fence which he wanted to repair. After hours of explaining all the different ways it could be fixed, he asked my opinion. 'What do you think is the best way?' he asked.

'It doesn't matter how it's repaired as long as it's strong and matches the rest of the fence,' I said. He kept me awake for half the night talking about it until finally I went to sleep.

In the middle of the night, when I heard Sophie crying, I got up to feed her. As I was holding the baby, Vincent suddenly grabbed me by the neck as if he intended to strangle me. I could not understand why he was so angry with me. 'You knew all along which way the fence should be repaired,' he said in his accusing tone, twisting his mouth in a cruel grimace. 'You wouldn't let on because you just wanted me to rack my brains unnecessarily.'

I was horrified that he had attacked me in this way while I was holding the baby. He then ordered me to keep the bedside lamp switched on for the rest of the night to stop me from going back to sleep. This attack, together with one other incident, set me thinking again about the advice which Dr Green had given me. Without sleep it was difficult to get my act together. If I was to try again either to leave home or to get Vincent forcibly admitted to hospital, it would have to be done meticulously with no margin for error.

One other memorable incident occurred after I had gone to bed early to try to catch up on sleep. I had left the landing light on, which Vincent had interpreted as a signal to the outside world. Then, as I climbed into bed, I heard the sound of breaking glass outside in the street as if someone was smashing bottles on the pavement. Vincent stormed upstairs and picked up the alarm clock. He pressed it hard against my face. 'You'd better watch your step or I'll put you in hospital,' he threatened, his unflinching stare gluing me to the pillow. I felt panic stricken but again was unable to put up any resistance. To run out of the house to call the police would have left the children in a vulnerable position and would also have run the risk of pushing Vincent over the edge. As usual it was a matter of submitting and waiting for him to calm down. So much for what he had said not so long ago—that he would sooner smash something up than hurt me. The reality felt very different. I was far from convinced that he could control himself.

First thing the following morning, while Vincent was still sleeping, I got Andy and Sophie ready and went to the public call box round the corner to call the police. I rang the emergency number and was put through to an officer. When I explained what had happened, the officer told me to contact our GP to arrange a home visit. Feeling disheartened, I explained that I feared this would not work after two previous bungled attempts.

'Well we can't just come and drag away a husband every time a wife phones up with a story like this' was his response. 'When we're called in we have to have the patient examined by a psychiatrist before any action can be taken.'

'But he's already been assessed by several psychiatrists, and the advice I was given by them was to call the police if I felt afraid.'

'If he's calmed down, there's nothing we can do.'

'What does it take then? A pool of blood?' I asked feeling agitated.

'Basically we can intervene only when he's in the act of being violent.'

'Oh, forget it!' I exclaimed putting down the phone. I felt angry and let down all over again. So much for Dr Green's advice! Did any of these people realize how impossible it was to implement their advice? Yet again I was back to square one.

I called at the baker's to buy a loaf before going home in case I needed a pretext for leaving the house. Vincent was still asleep when we got home, unaware that we had left the house for a while. It would have been impossible to discuss my fears with him. The only option was deception. Feeling crushed but needing to keep my feelings contained and concealed put a terrible strain on me. I put the radio on. They were playing Duran

Duran's song, 'Don't say a prayer for me now. Save it for the morning after.' These violent episodes gave new poignancy to the words and emotion of the song. It was all I could do to stem the tears. But looking after the children helped me to feel grounded.

There were further episodes. One afternoon Vincent came home after a visit to the post office to cash a giro—a money transfer. He accused me of taking his driver's licence, which he needed as proof of identity. 'I know you've taken it to stop me cashing the giro,' he said angrily.

'This makes no sense. The money is for both of us,' I replied.

I helped him to look for the driver's licence and went outside to the car to see if it had fallen out of his pocket. When I came back inside I started looking under the sofa and cushions. At this point he grabbed me by the neck with both hands and banged my head several times hard against the arm of the sofa. This left me feeling dazed, shaken, angry, and humiliated as well as very afraid. Afterwards I found the driver's licence on the shelf, which was where he normally kept it. Yet he was still firmly convinced that the whole incident was a planned operation designed to cause him aggravation. As usual, he showed not the slightest remorse or concern for me and gave no apology.

Now each time Vincent struck out at me or smashed something I could feel my resolve strengthen. The hold he had had over me was weakening. This hold was mainly the fact that I knew he was still acutely ill. Though the physical effects of his attacks left me mainly with bruises, they could easily result in more serious injury. Together with the emotional stress, this cruelty was again proving to be more than I was prepared to tolerate. I desperately needed to get things clearly in perspective. The thought that he needed me became overshadowed by the fact that the children needed me far more. I needed to protect them from his monstrous onslaughts.

Andy had already witnessed so much aggression. There were times when he looked to me for help when I myself felt crippled with fear and inertia. I felt so ashamed to stand by and watch Vincent punish him for trivial reasons. The worst part was that, after frightening him with his foul temper, he would order him in his threatening tone to stop crying. The poor child would stand there swallowing his sobs and trying to get his breathing under control. Although at first I tried to justify this by thinking of Vincent's parenting style as being strictly disciplinarian, I now feared that the forced suppression could have a damaging psychological effect, and I strongly disapproved of the smacking. Knowing how terrifying Vincent could be to me when he was angry, how much more terrifying would he be to a small child! It also disturbed me that Andy was witnessing too much of Vincent's aggression and violence towards me. In time Sophie would also be affected.

Now that Sophie was five months old, Vincent played with her sometimes but did not get involved very much with looking after her. He started to put pressure on me to stop breastfeeding and move her on to bottle feeding. I could see no point in doing this until she was ready. She showed no interest in taking the bottle, and I felt it was simply unnecessary to force her. Vincent was so adamant that he once took her and tried to force her to take a bottle. The poor baby struggled and spluttered in protest as he kept pushing the bottle back in her mouth. In the end he gave up. 'You'll have a real problem with her when the time comes to change over,' he said as a warning.

'I'll speak to the health visitor about it then,' I responded.

At the very mention of this, Vincent flew into a rage, and before I knew what was happening he had me in a stranglehold. 'Don't you dare talk to anybody about what goes on in this house! Do you hear me?' He tightened his grip into a vice. I was unable to breathe or speak. 'You lot push me too far and turn me into a raving lunatic. And I'll not give you any warning. You hear? I'll just kill somebody. And you'd better watch your step because it could be you.'

Then he loosened his grip and stormed off leaving me quivering and thinking harder and more seriously than ever before about the dangerous position I was in. It was never a case any more of simply being careful and avoiding confrontations. Without any provocation, he accused me too often of indicating things to him, of watching him, and of trying to belittle him.

Vincent went out, taking Andy with him. I just wanted to pick up the phone and talk to someone. I felt a desperate need to find someone I could confide in—not a doctor, social worker, or health visitor, but a friend. I thought about the women I had met at the playgroup. Chris had some health problems of her own, so it seemed inappropriate to burden her. Val struck me as the best bet. She seemed to be serious and sympathetic as well as cautious and reserved. Unfortunately, she had been away visiting her mother for a few weeks, so I had not seen her recently. We had exchanged phone numbers so that she could let me know when her son's birthday party was going to be. Andy had been invited, and we were looking forward to it. I decided that when she returned I would confide in her.

Next Vincent went through another phase of having difficulty sleeping. One evening before he was due to see his new GP, I said he should mention the problem to her, and he agreed. The next day I could scarcely believe it when he came home with a prescription for tablets, which had been recommended to him weeks ago at the counselling centre. At last I felt there was a chance that the tablets could be the medication that would treat his paranoia and other symptoms of schizophrenia. Suddenly it seemed as if, after all, things could be resolved. Maybe I could stop having to consider leaving home again. Maybe, just maybe, if his aggression subsided, Vincent and I could become reunited.

Vincent kept his tablets in his trouser pocket making sure that I never caught sight of them. He would not tell me what they were. At first I was afraid that he would refuse to take them. The next night he slept well. During the following weekend he relaxed, and we spent some time with the children. He agreed not to continue with the work outside until the weekend was over.

Monday came round and he resumed his work outside. It appeared that he was taking the tablets, but I could not be sure, and I certainly could not pressure him. He seemed to be in a difficult mood, and there followed a very restless night during which he kept me awake for a long time. Andy had caught another cold, which gave Vincent the impression that someone was making him catch one cold after another. When Andy kept waking up and coming into our bedroom, I kept putting him back in his own bed. After repeated attempts to settle him back to sleep, Vincent flew into a rage and accused me of preventing himself from sleeping. The next day he ordered me not to take Andy to the playgroup, saying he would have to stay home until he recovered from his cold. I wanted to take him to the park with me. It was a mild day, Andy wanted to come with me, and I thought the fresh air would do him good. Vincent was losing patience with my protests, and for once I was showing my agitation. Finally, tired of treading on eggshells to appease him, I let my feelings slip out. 'Why do you have to make our lives such a misery?' I exclaimed. At this Vincent picked up Andy's heavy wooden truck, hesitated for a second as if to choose the correct angle for the blow, and then wham! He smashed it against the side of my body catching my arm, which I held out to protect myself. My whole body quivered uncontrollably as the stinging pain in my arm and side kept me locked in a curled-up position. Andy sat and watched as Vincent then grabbed a handful of my hair, pulling it hard. He started lecturing me about all the work he had done on the house, all for our benefit, and vented his outrage at my comment. I tried to calm him down by telling him how irritable I felt after another sleepless night.

With that blow he destroyed any tattered remnants of love or care that I still felt for him. All that was now left was increasing resentment and hatred for his repeated acts of cruelty. If I stayed much longer in that house, I would risk losing control and picking up a knife myself to put an end to this torture.

That same afternoon I took Sophie to the clinic for her vaccination and check-up. I told the health visitor what had happened and arranged to return at a later date to show her my bruises again when they showed up more clearly. I realized this would serve as further evidence of Vincent's physical abuse, having learned that it was wise not to leave such things to chance. I might need evidence at some point in the future. I told her I wondered if I ought to speak to Vincent's doctor to let her know how bad things were at home and to ask what Vincent's tablets were. The health visitor supported this wholeheartedly and said she would try to contact the doctor first herself to put her in the picture.

As soon as I had the opportunity I rang Vincent's GP.

'I hear he's been knocking you about,' she said, getting straight to the point.

'Yes, I really need your advice,' I said. 'Have you received his medical records?'

'They've just come in the post today, but I haven't had chance to look at them yet.'

I explained to the doctor as briefly as possible the process we had been through, including Vincent's admission to hospital, his refusal of medication, and his current counselling sessions.

She was very direct with her advice. 'It's a terrible thing to have to say, but if things are as bad as you describe, why don't you leave home?'

I told her about the extensive work he had done on the house and about my hope that Vincent might change if only he could be treated with the right medication.

'You can't make a leopard change his spots,' she remarked with a poignancy that struck a reverberating chord.

It transpired that the tablets she had prescribed were merely tranquillizers and therefore would be of little long-term use. The doctor went on to explain that, even if he took them regularly, they would have no effect on his symptoms of schizophrenia.

'I can't do anything to treat him properly until he himself asks me for help. This is the way the legal procedures operate. I've spoken to your GP, Dr King, who said he'd be delighted to see you.'

'Please read his medical records carefully,' I asked. 'Don't on any account let Vincent know that I've been in contact with you. I can't emphasise enough how important this is, as he will take it out on me.'

'Don't worry about that. If you feel you want to talk again, give me a call.'

After this conversation, I realized even more clearly that, not only was I fighting a losing battle by trying to get Vincent help, but that the absurdity of the hideous system was being overlooked by all the health professionals responsible. It seemed to me that the legal procedures were almost as crazy as the illness itself. How could someone suffering from paranoid schizophrenia be expected to ask for treatment, when his total lack of insight into his own illness was a very feature of the condition? How could I be expected to get Vincent sectioned when he would hold me responsible for this for the rest of our lives? Why should my life be put in jeopardy? How many other carers were out there struggling like me to find a solution? How many families were caught up in this untenable situation? How many sufferers' mental health requirements were being seriously neglected?

Later on while I was out shopping, I called in at the health clinic so that I could get my bruises witnessed. They were now showing in stark black and blue. Vincent paid not the slightest attention to them. He simply pointed out that I was lucky to still have a head on my shoulders, which, quite apart from the implicit serious threat, was a really irritating expression that he used all too often.

At the end of the winter the weather was very wet. Often I would lie awake at night crying soft tears like the raindrops on the window. Because of the weather, Vincent took a break from the outdoor work he had started. The work he tackled next was to renew the joists under the wooden floor in the back room in the basement. They had been weakened by the effects of the damp after the flood during the thunderstorm from hell. Once again, he involved me in a lot of consultation about the way the work should be carried out. While he was in the process of repairing the floor, he soon got sidetracked into replacing other features in the room, which seemed totally unnecessary. This included removing shelves and a cupboard and re-routing the plumbing from the sink. Sometimes I would find a tool left lying by the phone as if to represent a threat. I would casually take it downstairs to him.

'Here. You left your hammer upstairs.'

'Oh did I really?' he would reply sarcastically.

As much as I tried to leave decisions up to him, he still involved me in endless discussion and finally blamed me for leading him astray and making him do things wrong. I wondered if he would continue to blame me if I left home and was no longer even there.

Chapter 15

Making the Break

The winter finally turned into spring, and the weather began to improve. One afternoon while Vincent was working outside, Val rang up to tell me the date of her son's birthday party. 'How are you all?' she asked.

'Actually I have a really serious problem that I feel desperate to talk to someone about,' I disclosed, leaving her the option to tell me if she had enough problems of her own at this point in time. 'The trouble is I don't know who to talk to. I've been wondering if you might be the right person for me to discuss the matter with.'

'I don't know either if I'd be the right person, but I'm willing to help if I can.'

Her response came as a relief. We arranged to meet in the park to walk our dogs. To my amazement and further relief, Val told me she knew a bit about paranoid schizophrenia and seemed to understand immediately the seriousness of my situation. She told me that she had once known a man who was extremely aggressive and very frightening as well as unpredictable.

'I've reached the point where I feel I simply have to leave him,' I explained. 'But I need to plan it very carefully without letting Vincent know.'

'It's unfortunate for him that you can't tell him, but I understand that it's probably the only thing you can do. You have to put the children first. I'm sure they must be deeply affected by the problems at home, so it's essential to get them away from him as soon as possible.'

We arranged to meet again, all being well, at the same time the following day. For once, fortune seemed to be on my side. We met again as planned in the park.

'I've talked to my husband, Dave, about you,' said Val. 'He agrees with me and thinks it's too unsafe for you to stay.'

'The only time we'd be able to leave is a Wednesday afternoon while Vincent is out for his counselling session.'

'I'll ask Dave if he can help you to move out some of your things. His friend has a van.'

I felt overwhelmed by this offer. As well as moral support and encouragement, they were also offering practical help, far exceeding my expectations.

My decision was now as firm as steel. Each time that Vincent did something to spite me, I now felt stronger, and my fear changed to concealed, seething anger. Naturally I had to be very careful not to reveal my true feelings. During the week that followed, I started to prepare in my mind exactly how I would carry out my meticulous plan. It was to be executed with military precision. I was forced into the role of actress and scheming collaborator. It was the very role that Vincent had cast for me anyway. I had to force myself to eat, smile, and look relaxed whenever Vincent was around. When he was out of sight, I would be wringing my hands and pacing up and down. I was living on adrenalin again, but in a different and more controlled and purposeful way compared to before.

At night, between snatching a couple of hours sleep, I planned the detailed timing of the operation and decided which belongings to take. Vincent would leave at 4:30 and be back by 6:30, allowing me two hours to execute the plan, though I could not take any chances in case he might come back early. I tried to work out how long it would take to pack and carry my things out of the house. Before this, I set a deadline by which all the baby's nappies would be washed and dried. We had no suitcases left, so I decided to use plastic bin liners. I had worked out that plates, cutlery, and saucepans would fit into the kitchen waste bin.

In a way, the task had been made easier by the fact that Vincent had already thrown away so many of my possessions. It was a case of selecting basic essentials. We had so little money left that I had to try to take as much as I could to make life that much easier once we managed to start afresh. I wished I could have started to sort things out in advance such as toys, documents, and the children's clothes, but this was out of the question as the slightest thing would arouse Vincent's already heightened suspicions. I did not allow myself to think too much about Suki, Bullet, and Bailey or how Vincent might behave towards them. I loved the animals, but I had to remain focused. It would tear me apart if I allowed myself to get emotional about leaving them.

I felt terribly afraid that the plan would fail and go terribly wrong. I wondered if I was being greedy by hoping to take so many things. Yet I remembered how depressing it had felt when we had spent two days at the homeless unit. If I could I would take the sofa bed, which, as it consisted merely of lumps of foam, was easy to carry. Other essentials included bedclothes, the pram, a few kitchen utensils, a bag of toys, and clothes. Then, if it was not too much trouble for Dave and his friend, and if there was space in the van, I would like to have the tumble drier and the washing machine. It would be difficult to afford disposable nappies and to replace all the items that I was to leave behind. Vincent would take the car when he went to his appointment. He would have the other sofa, table, TV, fridge, and freezer. He would also have the remains of our savings. There would be no grounds for him to complain that I was being unfair. He had the comfort of the house as well as the convenience of the car.

This time it had to be absolutely final with no return visits to fetch things. There would be no more opportunity for me to change my mind, and certainly no opportunity for Vincent to get at the children or threaten suicide. This way I would not have to face the pets that I had to abandon. My first move after he left for his appointment would be to phone Val and take the children quickly to her house in the pram. Vincent had never met Val and Dave and did not know where they lived. It would be a ten-minute walk with the pram. I could then run back home and start packing.

Val and I met again to plan the finer details. She would be able to store some of my belongings for me. She had made enquiries for me about Women's Aid and advised me to go to them for help with accommodation rather than to social services. I planned to contact them as soon as we had left the house. Beyond that it was difficult to make further plans. Although to date Vincent had not missed any of his counselling appointments, I was aware that he could suddenly decide to stay home or even insist on taking Andy with him.

Shortly before the deadline, I made one more visit to the health visitor. I told her that I had made up my mind to leave home. For the first time she told me she thought I was doing the right thing. 'Quite honestly, I don't know how you've managed to stick it out this long,' she said candidly. 'I think the children are bound to be affected by the tensions at home. Could you contact the social worker in charge of your case to let her know too?'

I had still never met this social worker. I phoned her while Vincent took Andy to the barber's, but our conversation was cut short when Vincent returned home earlier than expected. She had just been in the process of offering me help to move out my belongings.

The evening before our planned exodus, Vincent suddenly decided we should go out to eat instead of me cooking. Andy was still asleep on the sofa having a late afternoon nap. When Vincent woke him to get him ready, it was clear that he was still sleepy and did not want to go out. We fell back on our normal routine of picking up a takeaway and bringing it home to eat. As we sat in front of the TV, for a moment it struck me that this was to be our last supper together, and I found it increasingly difficult to keep the dreaded lump in my throat under control. Then suddenly Vincent pounced on Andy who was innocently in the process of pulling the cover off the TV guide. Vincent shook him violently threatening to smack him. This was sufficient to wrench me out of any more sentimental feelings. *Just a few more hours*, I told myself.

Since the first time I had taken the children and left home, just before Christmas, Vincent must have been aware of the possibility that it could happen again. Once, some time before we had left, he had accused me of scheming to leave. I understood this to be the reason he often took Andy with him when he went out. There were times when he would get angry with me and say, 'Why don't you just take the baby and go?' I told him that I could never leave without both children and that they needed to grow up together as brother and sister. I even said I would not leave without the pets. Then he would challenge my reason for assuming that I had the right to keep the children. It was very difficult to help him understand why I felt that I had more right than he did. He would flare up if I told him he was ill, unstable, or disturbed. All I could say was that, if absolutely necessary, I felt perfectly confident that I could bring them both up by myself. Having spent so much of his own childhood without having his father around, I think that Vincent had become very anxious about the prospect of his own son facing the same fate. The fact that his mother had not been around either did not seem to matter to him. He did not ever express the same concern about having responsibility for Sophie's upbringing. He gave the impression that he would be quite satisfied with dividing the children: he would keep Andy, and I would keep Sophie.

As for the pets, he had issued me with a stern warning: 'If you ever decide to leave home again, make sure you don't leave any pets behind or else I'll have them all put to sleep.' I did not take this warning seriously and thought he would be glad of their company. I could not be sure, but I resigned myself to the fact that, for practical reasons, I would have to leave them behind. He had said these things based on hypothetical reasoning. When it came down to the reality of the situation, I thought that he would feel differently. Yet I was aware of how heartless he had been when he had left Bullet out in the cold for hours on the doorstep when I had been admitted to hospital. At the best of times he showed very little affection for Bailey, whose temperament was completely different to Bullet's. Whereas Bullet had a placid nature, Bailey was highly strung. Whereas in the park Bullet was a wanderer, Bailey liked to guard the children and stay near us. Although the dogs seemed jealous if one got more attention than the other, I thought they would miss each other if they were separated. I thought they would find some comfort in each other's company after we had left.

Over the last nine months of his illness Vincent had definitely developed an aversion to Suki, our Siamese cat. In preparation for our final exit, I therefore tried to find someone to take her. It was Chris who said she knew someone interested and willing, so I arranged to take the cat over the road to her flat on Wednesday provided everything went according to plan. In time I hoped that somehow I might see my pets again or even be in a position to repossess them.

At one time when Vincent had accused me of scheming to leave him, there had been no immediate foundation for his accusations, so I had flatly denied them. Well before I had made new friends at the playgroup, he had often made accusations that I had a group of friends giving me support and advice. He would make terrible threats and jeer at me.

'Go and tell your friends,' he would say. My response was that such threats did not bear being repeated to anyone. I denied having friends or getting help from any source. I felt as though he expected to be able to break me down mentally as if in retaliation, or maybe he was simply projecting his own fears. Other times I would have to admit that his behaviour towards me made me feel like running away, but that I had nowhere to run to, and besides, running away would not solve anything.

Now that I had decided to leave, I wanted to put the record straight by leaving him a note. I wrote it hastily while I was in the park and kept it hidden until it was time to leave.

Dear Vincent,

I don't expect you to understand why I've decided to leave, but I'll try to explain anyway. The fact is that I'm frightened of you and can't stand your violence any more. I'm sorry to have to leave while you're out, but there's no way I could have told you. Don't worry about the children. I'll take good care of them. I'm sorry I've had to leave the dogs, but I've found a home for Suki.

I'll write again once I've got things sorted out.

Nicki

Finally the day came. It was the first Wednesday in April. I hoped that a Wednesday would prove to be luckier than Fridays had turned out to be in my previous attempts to leave. Vincent spent the morning working on the fireplace in the basement, stripping off plaster and resetting loose bricks. The time for his appointment approached. He asked me to give him a hand to clear up so that he could get ready to leave. When we had finished cleaning up, I went upstairs to feed Sophie. I was still breastfeeding, and it was important for my timing to get this done before he set off.

Vincent left on schedule. It was time for action. In accordance with my plan, I hastily got Andy and Sophie ready and made my phone call to Val. Without delay I ran as fast as I could pushing them both in the pram at a speed they had never before experienced. I arrived at the same time Dave's friend arrived with the van and another of his friends. What a welcome sight! So we had two cars and a van. We drove to the house, parked outside, and got started. Within minutes there were plastic bin liners all over the house. I kept the dogs in one of the bedrooms out of the way. The men carried the big stuff out first and loaded the van while I filled the bags and shouted out directions. Then I remembered the cat. I gave instructions to one of the men to take her to Chris across the road. I asked the friend with the van if it would be possible for me to take the washing machine. He fiddled for what seemed like an age to disconnect it, but could not find the stopcock to turn the water off.

'If you can't do it just leave it,' I said. The last thing I wanted was to run the risk of Vincent turning up and going berserk. I would gladly sacrifice my ultimate desire to keep the washing machine. Finally he managed to disconnect the machine but could not stop the trickle of water coming from the connecting pipe. Fortunately we were able to divert the water into a floor vent to prevent the water from accumulating.

I finished packing crockery wrapped in tea towels, dusters, and clothes into buckets and the kitchen waste bin. Then I went down to the basement to fetch my documents. Not forgetting to leave the note I had written beside the phone, I quickly looked through the address book and ripped out the pages that contained my family's details. I had already copied out details of other phone numbers and addresses I would need. I was adamant that Vincent should have no contact with my family. We still had about forty-five minutes to spare. Dave was looking nervous, obviously eager to get away at the earliest opportunity. He told me that, as he had been unloading his car, Sophie had not stopped crying the whole time. With no time to hug the dogs or clear up the trail of mess, let alone to glance over my shoulder at the house, I left with them like a shot. We just got the hell out of there as fast as we could.

Sophie calmed down as soon as I was finally able to hold her in my arms. Andy had been fine playing happily with Val's son. We stored all our bulky items in the hallway at Val and Dave's house. After a meal together, I phoned the Women's Aid organization. The only centre with a vacant room was twenty miles away. Although I would have loved to stay close to Val and Dave, I felt happier at the prospect of a safe distance between us and Vincent. Dave drove us straight away to the place, and I thanked him effusively for all his help. I had realized, late but not too late, the value of true friends. I felt deeply indebted to them and hoped that, if I was unable to repay them in kind, at least eventually I might be able to help others in their hour of need just as I had been helped in mine.

Chapter 16

Moving On

The sense of complete freedom was absolutely exhilarating. I had not realized the extent to which Vincent's domination had penetrated every aspect of my life. It did not take long to adapt to our new situation free from his iron grip. I could buy whatever brand I pleased of sugar, biscuits, coffee, or bread without needing to consider the colour of the packaging. Neither did I have to avoid using plastic carrier bags because the colour sent secret signals to the neighbours. I was free to go to bed at eight o'clock without disturbances and crazy conversations keeping me awake for hours. I could leave items out 'on display' without fear of any paranoid reaction. I could enjoy my time with the children. If I chose to, I could buy cheap, second-hand goods of inferior quality. I could go out as often as I liked, for as long as I liked, with whomever I liked. In short, I could organize my own life and make my own decisions without any need to consult or surrender to him as his prey. The only restrictions on my freedom were the Women's Aid rules of the house and my childcare responsibilities, which I gladly accepted.

One of the first things I did was to buy a new camera. I took loads of photographs of Andy and Sophie. They were so adorable. After Vincent had thrown away my photo album, I needed to start a new collection to capture the children while they were small. In time I was able to retrieve from my sister and parents some of the photos of Andy when he was a baby. All had not been lost after all as a result of Vincent's purges.

Already accustomed to living on a limited income, I found it no real hardship to manage on welfare benefits. What I missed were the comforts of our home—our pets, the use of the car, and the familiarity of our local park. It took a long time to get used to being alone in the evenings, though being on my own was a massive improvement to being trapped in an abusive relationship. I still felt a sense of dread that Vincent might find out where we were. I imagined that, if ever he found us, the danger would be much more acute than ever. Yet my feelings also included a deep sense of tragedy, similar to the sadness I had felt once before when we had left home. Though this time the sadness was less acute, it had a finality about it. During the time after Vincent's illness had taken possession of him, starting well before Sophie was born, I had experienced something like a long, drawn-out bereavement. Our marriage had been totally devastated by his psychological condition. It had been flogged to death.

Now that I was able to talk freely about the ordeal I had been through, I was able to regain my trust in people. Several people I spoke to told me about close relatives and friends who suffered from various forms of schizophrenia. I read one book after another on the subject. Now I could talk about the condition using the proper terminology. I could analyse aspects in terms of social maladjustment, delusional episodes, relapses, and prognoses. Although it is a mystifying illness that defies logical explanation and rational understanding, it is clear that there are many symptoms and manifestations which different sufferers have in common. I found this very strange. Just as Dr Green had pointed out to me, the books reported that there was no cure. Neither was there definitive information on its causes. After sharing Vincent's nightmares and torments at close quarters for such a long time, I felt relieved that I had finally been given no choice but to leave him. If the sufferer is a son, daughter, parent, or sibling, the burden of responsibility could be so much worse; you cannot divorce your child, your mother, or your brother. It was clear that, without medication, Vincent would be very likely to suffer a series of further serious relapses.

In terms of the struggle for him to gain insight into his own condition, it had been a completely hopeless case. Sometimes he felt that people were forcing him to learn something he did not wish to know about. He felt that everyone else was in collusion over a secret of how things should be done, yet no one would tell him directly what he was supposed to do. At other times he interpreted the confusion in his mind as a game that people were playing with him, making him feel manipulated and tormented. He wrestled with these notions, unable to realize that he had lost his grip on reality. His capacity for decision making was very seriously impaired, leaving him heavily reliant on my advice, which almost always backfired on me in the form of crazed accusations.

Soon after leaving home, I contacted a solicitor to begin divorce proceedings in order to gain legal custody of the children. I wrote to Vincent to explain more fully my reasons for leaving and for taking legal action. The solicitor arranged for letters to be sent from her address. Vincent wrote back to me via my solicitor. His first letter was angry, as if to say, 'Good riddance to the lot of you!' His next few letters were full of promises and pleas for us to come back home. Eventually it became clear from his letters that he could never understand my reasons for leaving. He continued to refuse to accept that there was anything wrong with him. He still held me responsible for everything that had gone wrong. His false belief about me was unshakable, even though he stood to lose everything dear to him. I learned that such fixed beliefs are also a feature of the illness. In my final letter to him, I tried to explain this to him and the fact that no one could be held responsible. It was his illness—paranoid schizophrenia—that was the root cause of our broken marriage. I never received any further reply.

That strange recurring dream that had disturbed me now seemed like a subconscious premonition of what was to happen. The sense of neglect that had troubled me in the dream was now evident in reality, as well as the emotion associated with a sudden loss of contact. This original recurring dream was now to be replaced by a different one of a retrospective nature. The new dream is one in which I find myself still trapped in a marriage with Vincent. Mostly the dream fills me with a sense of dread, but at other times it rekindles the close connection we enjoyed during the early years of our relationship. For a short time in the dream, I feel a warm sense of intimacy and security, before I realize in a panic that I absolutely need to get away from him. I believe that this dream reflects the conflicting emotions which inevitably arise when you are wrenched away from someone you once loved very deeply. With both these dreams, it is as if my subconscious mind plays tricks on me by immersing me in a time warp. I wake up needing to surface from the depths of the past and reorient myself in the present.

For weeks I spent a long time reflecting on what had happened, pouring over our years together and speculating about different possible outcomes. I spent many hours staring into space. If any music playing evoked a melancholy mood, I would struggle to hold back the tears. Yet even if I had felt compelled to stay with Vincent, I was convinced that I would no longer be able to help him. My absence provided him with a fresh start and an opportunity to meet new people in the way that he had planned after we had left him in December. Maybe my very presence had merely served as an aggravation, even though it felt as if I was being used as a scapegoat. Though these thoughts conflicted with my sense of duty to him as his wife, I did not torment myself with feelings of guilt. I had absolutely no reason to regret having children with Vincent. I doted on Andy and Sophie. They meant everything to me.

The spring sunshine was uplifting. It was wonderful to go out with the children every day. I made friends with the other women in the shared house. We were able to stay for about six weeks. Some of them had similar stories to tell about their partners' mental illness, drug abuse, or alcoholism causing violent reactions. All of us had escaped from being victims of physical and mental abuse.

The next step would be to consider where we would make our permanent home or next temporary abode. Returning to the area where we had lived before was clearly not an option. The prospect of being placed in a council flat in a monstrous block in this area of Outer London was not a choice that I was prepared to consider. I instructed my solicitor to arrange for our house to be put on the market. It was a difficult decision in view of all the work that Vincent had done to transform it. In 1976 we had paid £9,500 for the house. Now in 1983, as a luxury home, it would be worth at least three times that price. In addition to the increase in value due to improvements to the house, London property values had risen sharply in the previous seven years. With my share of the proceeds from the sale, I would be able to put down a sizeable deposit on a house or flat and get back to work so that I would be eligible for a mortgage.

A couple of weeks after we left home, I decided to contact my sister and mother to start to tell them what had happened. I did not relish the prospect of being told, 'We told you so!' But I was prepared to face this response whether it was articulated or not. When I phoned again another week later my sister could hardly contain her excitement.

'I've found you a small house to rent!' she announced. 'It's only about a mile from our house in the village. If you want it, I'll make all the arrangements. Just let me know when to expect you and we'll be there to meet you at the station.' The safe distance from London was a big factor in convincing me to accept her offer of help. The other main factor was the advantage to Andy and Sophie of regular contact with their grandparents, aunt, uncle, and two cousins. This would build badly needed stability into their young lives. It would also provide me with an opportunity to recuperate while the solicitor worked from a distance on the sale of the house and the custody proceedings. Once again I found myself feeling deeply indebted. There was a warm glowing feeling about having family to fall back on. My sister helped us in so many practical ways and with such eagerness that I felt she fully enjoyed the whole process. She was indeed delighted to help us out.

Before we left London, we had a few social engagements to attend. First there was the birthday party Val had invited us to. Her son was now three—five months older than Andy. We took a long bus ride and joined in the fun of the festivities. We also accepted an invitation to another children's party at Tom and Cindy's, Val and Dave's friends. I had met Cindy a few times at the playgroup, as their son and daughter were close in age to Andy and Sophie. It was her husband, Tom, who had helped Dave to move my belongings out of the house. I wondered what they must have thought of me as I was feeling so destitute that day when we left home. On another sunny day Val, Cindy, and I took all the children to Crystal Palace Park for a lovely picnic. We all took photos to capture the moment. I explained that I would be moving up to the Midlands and would arrange collection of all the bulky items that had been kept safely stored for us— something for which I was extremely grateful. I promised to keep in touch.

A removal van transported our belongings up the M1 motorway as I travelled with Andy and Sophie by train. On arrival my sister and niece were there to meet us at the station. Andy was now aged two and nine months. It was the first time they had seen Sophie, who was seven months old. We were greeted with genuine affection, and it was difficult to believe that we had been relatively estranged for so many years. I was relieved that they spared me an interrogation, leaving me the option to volunteer bits and pieces at a time about the ordeal we had been through.

The little end of terrace property perched on the edge of the narrow pavement with only three or four feet between its frontage and the busy main road. A thin slice of a house, it had one front window upstairs and one downstairs next to the flimsy front door. Beside the house was a red brick railway bridge carrying coal freight from the local coal mine to the power station a few miles away. Opposite was a friendly fish and chip shop which we were to take full advantage of—one serving of fish and chips was more than sufficient for all three of us. There was a red telephone box on the corner a short distance away which was also to prove to be very convenient. An infants' school with a nursery was situated a short walk away, and the main shopping centre was less than a mile further along the road.

The tiny rented house was very basic, but my sister had helped to furnish it with enough items for it to feel like home, at least for a few months. She even got me an antique sewing machine similar to the one Vincent had thrown out. We had a long rear garden where my brother-in-law laid some turf so that the children would have a lawn to play on. Beyond that lay a vegetable plot where I soon planted vegetables from assorted seeds with variable success.

We spent most Sundays at my parents' and most Wednesday afternoons at my sister's. She would also call in often to visit us when she was passing. I renewed contact with spidery Ray who used to visit us when he came up from London to see his folks who lived just a few miles away. We had some lovely days out exploring the woods with him and his new puppy, a hyperactive Welsh border collie called Polly. Ray had separated from Carol, his American wife, some years before, so we commiserated with one another over our respective separations.

I soon made friends with some of the mothers of young children who lived in the neighbourhood by attending a local mother and toddler group.

Even though Sophie was still a baby, she and Andy played together well. Andy was impressed with her physique as he was under the misapprehension that her chubby arms were endowed with strong muscles. He loved to play games based on the He-Man television character with Sophie playing along taking an active non verbal role.

One day we had a welcome visit from Tom and Cindy with their two children, as they were passing through the area on their way to visit relatives further north. They told me their news that they were planning to move from London to Cornwall. It was another opportunity to enjoy the company of friends and take more photos of the children playing together in the garden.

Soon I bought a brand new bicycle with a child's seat and cycled everywhere until I could afford to buy an old car. I found a part-time teaching job and cycled four miles to a school in an outlying village two mornings a week, dropping Andy off at the free nursery close to the house and Sophie at a different one a mile away, which I had to pay for. Sometimes she would fall asleep in her seat as we cycled home. By this time I had lost the few extra pounds I had gained during my pregnancy. I felt physically very fit. Once a week I attended an evening class in beginners-level Spanish and I taught French to adults one evening a week at an Adult Education Institute. My parents offered to babysit one evening a week, and my niece the other evening.

Among the students at the Spanish class, I recognised the parents of an old school friend called Maria. Through them I renewed contact with Maria, who now had three young children and lived in Yorkshire. Eventually, after problems developed in her relationship with her partner, she moved with the children back to our hometown, leaving her partner. This provided yet another opportunity for me to realize that separation and divorce were far from uncommon. For a while I looked after her baby a couple of days a week while she went to work, also as a teacher of modern languages. She insisted on paying me for the child minding. I felt impressed and inspired by her determination to work full time while raising her three young children and sorting out a new home.

I bought a small portable black-and-white TV set. It was around this time that the Band Aid concert was shown on television. My niece would lend me cassettes to play including New Order, U2, Michael Jackson, and Madonna. Apart from this I relied on the radio to catch up with the latest musical developments.

That winter it was exceptionally cold. We had lots of snow and enjoyed making a snowman in the garden. I planted out our small, live Christmas tree. During the festive season I had put it in the cold front room so that it would be less likely to shed its needles. In the house it was so cold that we often had frost forming on the inside of the windows. The only rooms that had a gas fire were the living room and the front room, but I could afford to heat only one room. As there was no internal door fitted in the front room, the heat escaped immediately up the stairs, through the draughty sash widows, and through the wafer-thin front door. The bedrooms had no heating at all. I bought a second-hand, oil-filled radiator for the bathroom, which also heated the children's room on cold nights. How I missed central heating! Sometimes I ran out of money for the gas meter, but we managed on what meagre resources we had without resorting to borrowing money. I just kept remembering how life had been in my student days, which had not been so long ago.

Apart from the usual coughs and colds, the children endured the cold winter without any major health issues. Inevitably they picked up various ailments from mixing with other children. They both contracted chicken pox, and then Andy was also ill with the mumps. As his speech development was slow, I got his ears checked. He needed to be admitted to the local hospital to have grommets inserted to drain away excess fluid. He was very brave about spending a few days in hospital without me, though we visited him every day for as long as possible.

Life as a single parent was slowly taking off, but in the evenings when I was at home alone while the children were asleep I felt quite lonely. At first I used to feel really down at heart every time I saw young children out and about with their fathers. Although it felt good to get away from Vincent, there was a lingering sense of deprivation. Of course at this stage the children did not seem to feel this. At her tender age, Sophie was too young to have any awareness of any difference in the family circumstances or our living standards, and Andy simply accepted the change in our circumstances without question. Anxious to keep alive some memory of Vincent, I occasionally talked to him about his daddy. His reaction without being prompted would be, 'I don't like Daddy play fighting.'

It was during the first few months after we had moved away from London that I began to scribble my notes on the ordeal I had been through living with Vincent. I needed to do this while the memories were still relatively fresh in my mind. It soon became a compulsion to write so that I could shift the whole episode from my head on to paper. This way I did not have to keep talking so much about my experiences to different people. I bought a small typewriter and a set of notebooks. I began typing some of the notes, but it was an annoying and fiddling operation to make corrections, and especially bothersome to keep changing the ribbon. In the end I simply scribbled by hand, which was faster. If only there had been word processors or computers then! Although I found the process of writing therapeutic, I did not feel that the time was yet right to show people what I had written. I decided that, when Andy and Sophie were young teenagers, I would let them read my account so that they had a complete understanding of their father's condition and its effect on our lives.

Sophie was now one year old and walking. While my parents and sister were away on holiday I fell ill with a really bad case of the flu and could hardly move. It was then, when I could not even get myself out of bed in the night to feed Sophie, that I decided it was time to stop breastfeeding. The change was well timed as she was more than ready to feed from a bottle. She started talking at a very early age, and I used to record my conversations with the children on audio cassette tapes, as well as songs, crazy crashing of musical instruments, and the occasional bark from the dog. Yes, I had retrieved one of the dogs from Vincent!

A letter had come from my solicitor saying that Vincent had asked me to make arrangements to collect Bailey, who was proving to be a handful. I went to the call box to phone Val to ask if she would be willing to collect the dog and meet me at St Pancras Station so that I could bring her back to live with us. To my relief Val agreed. My parents looked after the children for the day. It was great to see Val again, albeit briefly, and to discover that she was expecting a second child. I could see that Bailey had lost a lot of weight, and she hardly seemed to recognise me. I brought her back with me on the train. She soon settled in with us and regained the weight that she had lost. However, she seemed more neurotic than ever, and I did not feel that I could entirely trust her around the children. At times she would bark repeatedly in the house while staring at me in a rather aggressive manner, as if to tell me about the ordeal that she had also been through.

Outside in the back garden she explored her new surroundings. Sometimes at night she used to get through the garden fence and find her way round to the front door with scratches all over her nose as if she had had an encounter with a hedgehog. Other times in the mornings, if the milkman had left the back gate open, she would slip out, and I would have to run out after her in my pyjamas and dressing gown to catch her before she ventured on to the busy road. There was a very friendly woman who lived nearby who adored English bull terriers. Every time she saw us out for our daily walk, she would stop for a chat and ask to stroke Bailey. She even offered to look after her any time we wanted to go away. That was a great help, as my sister and parents were definitely not dog lovers.

At Easter we had a fun holiday in Wales together with Maria and her children who respectively were aged one, two, three, four, and five. We stayed in self-catering accommodation a short distance from the sandy beach where the children were happy to play in the sand in spite of the cold wind. We also had a fun outing to Dovedale in the Derbyshire Dales exploring the hills and streams. At one point Andy wandered off and got lost. A stranger pointed at Maria in the distance and asked him, 'Is that your mummy?' He replied, 'No,' not thinking of saying she was actually his mummy's friend. Anyway we got him back, and then out of sheer devilment he pushed Sophie into the stream, and she had to borrow dry clothes belonging to Maria's son. That summer we even had a short holiday in Brussels. We stayed with an old university friend of mine who lived there working as a translator for the European Commission. He showed us round the local sights, and we all enjoyed a day out at a theme park. How lovely it was to catch up with my old friends and have so much fun with the children.

A friend I had met at the playgroup suffered really badly from postnatal depression, which made me realize how everybody had a fair share of problems. Knowing my situation, she asked if I would be interested in buying her beat-up old car. It was an attractive proposition, as the bike had its limitations, especially in the snow. I actually ended up paying less for the old car than I had for the new bike. Although covered in patches of rust, the car proved to be an extremely trustworthy vehicle, which we naturally called Rusty. Soon I was able to work four days a week for one term at a school in a neighbouring town ten miles away. This was temporary maternity cover. I honestly expected the car to fall apart as I bombed up and down the dual carriageway at high speed to get to work on time and back again to collect the children. However the car lasted long enough until I had saved enough money to buy a newer model in much better condition.

At Christmas we received a large parcel from Vincent via the solicitor. It contained a selection of very carefully wrapped packages in brightly coloured paper, so tastefully wrapped that I suspected to be out of character for Vincent. The lovely new clothes for the children were very welcome, as I could not afford many new clothes for them. As I removed the sticky tape, I pulled out a long blond hair. Had he already met someone else? I felt quite taken aback. If this was the case, it seemed like swift work; it had been only eight months since we had left home.

Ironically, our divorce proceedings were completed on Valentine's Day in 1984. Then the court hearing came up when I was required to testify against Vincent's claim for custody and access. The house was in the process of being sold. I asked for two-thirds of the share of the proceeds of sale on the grounds that Vincent was not paying maintenance for the children, that we would eventually need a three-bedroom house, and that I would have to provide for the children. His failure to pay maintenance indicated that he was unlikely to be working.

I had decided that the children should have no contact with him. I had been advised to deny access on the grounds that children risk adopting behaviour from a parent whose behaviour and thoughts are disturbed. I was very concerned about Vincent's unpredictability and violence, feeling that any risk was simply not worth taking. I received notice of an appointment with a health visitor who would be coming to check our accommodation and living conditions at our rented house. It was disconcerting when I imagined her making a similar assessment of Vincent in the luxurious surroundings of our London home.

I felt nervous about appearing in court and having to confront Vincent. When I saw him, he looked smart and proud to have his new partner, Lucy, by his side. She was an attractive blond woman and looked several years younger than I. I felt quite sickened by Vincent's apparent display of confidence and the sight of the radiant couple, as this risked mitigating the objections to allowing access which I was about to raise in my testimony. My impressions of the happy couple seemed to verify my theory that my leaving him might do him some good, enabling him to make a fresh start. I did not speak to the amorous pair, preferring to keep a surly distance.

In court it was announced that he had now remarried and moved in with Lucy and her two children from her previous marriage. I said my shaky piece about his illness, his violent aggression, and his disturbed, unpredictable behaviour. On the strength of his new family situation, the fact that he was now working, and the importance of Andy and Sophie having some contact with their father, he was granted supervised access for one afternoon a month. The other conditions were that he would have to be prepared to travel to a place in Nottingham where the access could be supervised, and that he paid a nominal amount of maintenance. It was made clear by the judge that, without access, children generally risked fantasising about their father.

I was amazed at the way that Vincent had managed to turn his life around, bounce back, and remarry already. Yet, after everything I had been told about the long-term prognosis of his illness, I had a strong suspicion that his recovery could not last long. On the other hand, I wondered if perhaps Vincent was now taking medication for his schizophrenia and if this was how he might have been able to recover from his symptoms. For the sake of the children and his new family, I sincerely hoped that this was the case. Otherwise, again for the sake of the children, I wished that I could somehow impose a requirement for him to accept medical treatment as a condition of my own; that is, as a condition for him to be granted access. I realized that this was an unrealistic idea, knowing how difficult it would be to enforce such a condition.

The supervised access visits took place as planned, and on the first occasion I was able to meet Lucy and her two children properly. They were very friendly, good humoured, and likeable. Lucy's son was about twelve years old and her daughter about nine. She had long blond hair so it must have been her hair that I had found in the Christmas wrapping. I even got to see Bullet, who had travelled with them, so while Vincent had access to the children, I had access to the dog and enjoyed taking him for a long walk. This was an unexpected bonus. The family lived outside London in the Surrey area. Vincent had a new car, which was much smarter than mine. And he looked well and very smart in his new clothes. It appeared that he was now working again and earning good money. The family seemed very happy together. It was a relief to me to know that I was no longer in such danger of being tracked down by Vincent. He now had other fish to fry.

After six months of supervised access, the situation was due to be reviewed. Provided all went smoothly, supervised access could lead to unsupervised access, which we could negotiate ourselves directly without the need to go through a solicitor or other intermediary. As long as Vincent appeared to be well, and as long as the children were in the new family setting, I felt more at ease about the prospect of eventual unsupervised access. I hoped that Lucy could see that I was a reasonable person. After all, if ever she was to find herself in a similar dilemma with Vincent and in need of support, I wanted to be there to help her.

Meanwhile, at last I was able to do Val and Dave a favour. After the birth of their daughter they needed someone to house sit and look after their dog while they went away on holiday. I thought it would be a good opportunity to see how it felt for us to spend time back in the South London area where we used to live. Leaving Bailey with the family who had offered to look after her, we took our shiny new brown car to London and settled into the house to look after Val and Dave's dog. It felt odd taking a different dog to the same park where I used to walk Bullet and Bailey. Most of the time I had to keep him on the lead as he was likely to cause arguments with other dogs. Ray came to visit. Carrying Sophie high up on his shoulders, he spent lots of time with us having fun in the parks. We enjoyed boat trips on the lake, picnics, and taking another look at the dinosaurs in Crystal Palace Park. The children always loved visits to the playground and running round playing with Polly, Ray's puppy who was growing up fast.

In spite of all my efforts to resettle back in my home town, I still felt that I did not belong there . . . that it was a temporary stopgap. The regular contact with my parents and my sister's family was important to us in terms of making up for lost time and establishing a closer rapport both with me and the children. They understood that I needed to get back to full-time work. I had been applying for full-time teaching jobs in the Midlands area. Although I was successfully short-listed for interviews, the candidates appointed were usually teachers already known to the schools. Now, during our week in London, I realized just how much I really missed living there in the capital with its international population and rich cultural life. By contrast, my home town felt again like a cultural wasteland. Above all, I missed the ethnic diversity of the local community.

I decided to apply for a job at a school in the London borough where my own reputation had already been well established. At my first interview I was successfully appointed as second in charge of the languages department. It was time to be reinstated on the professional ladder and to rebuild my career. It was a relatively small school which seemed to have a warm heart and soul. The staff were very friendly. After eighteen months away in my home town I was ready to make a comeback. It was the end of 1984—the end of another era and the start of a new one.

Chapter 17

Trucking

After advertising in the newspaper, I found a family interested in taking Bailey. She was still neurotic and difficult to trust with the children. The new family seemed to offer a suitable home for her and genuinely liked her. After taking some final photos, I handed her over. It would have been impossible to make the move back to London with a dog. We would have to stay in temporary accommodation until I was in a position to buy a permanent new home.

On New Year's Eve I loaded all our belongings, including the Christmas tree with roots intact, into the hired van and headed down the M1 motorway in the snow. It was the first time I had ever driven a large van. Listening to my new cassettes by Bryan Ferry and Tears for Fears helped to put me at more ease. Soon I felt like a real trucker, my mother having made me a flask of hot coffee and some sandwiches for the journey. I had left the children with my parents for the day. On arrival I deposited our belongings at Ray's one-bedroom flat and art studio in Clapham, which was already cluttered with his own belongings as well as his array of fascinating art materials. He had offered to let us stay there until I could get our house purchase arranged and move into a new home. I made a contribution to the rent and tried to keep the children from bothering him. We slept on a mattress on his kitchen floor and were woken each morning by the odd sensation of Polly licking our faces.

At incredibly short notice I sorted out a school place for Andy and a nursery place for Sophie close to where we used to live. I planted our Christmas tree in Ray's garden in the same plot where his own Christmas tree was growing. It was a very busy time for me. I needed time to study the set books for my A-level French literature class as well as to prepare materials and lesson plans for all the other classes on my timetable. The school used different textbooks to those I had been familiar with. Each morning I had to get the children ready early so that I could drop them off at the child minder's, who would take them to school. Then I would continue on my journey to my school.

The ground-floor flat was cramped for four of us, but it was only to be for a limited period. Soon, after looking round at several properties, I was able to put down a deposit on a small terraced house in a friendly back street close to Andy's school. It was a quiet street in the sense that there was little traffic, but as it was colonised by lots of children playing out, it was very lively. The row of houses was situated right beside the railway track, but it had a small back garden and felt homely. Whenever the trains rattled past, the house would shake to its foundations. A mid-terraced house in the middle of the row, it gave the impression that it could easily withstand the trauma from the trains as the houses supported each other. It was in a mixed community with several neighbouring households consisting of single-parent families. I felt that this close-knit community would help Andy and Sophie to grow up feeling secure. I also felt a sense of belonging there. Besides, I could only just afford a house and was adamant not to compromise by buying a flat. Every penny of the proceeds from my share of the sale of our marital home went towards the deposit.

Now that the access visits were able to take place, I would take the children alternate weekends to stay with Vincent and Lucy. Vincent would drop them back afterwards. Until we were able to move into our new home, staying with Ray helped me to feel as if I had some kind of a social life, even though it was piggybacking on his for a while. Many of Ray's friends were interesting artists and musicians. My new job kept me busy, and I soon made lots of new friends among the staff.

After five months in the flat it was clear that we had outstayed our welcome by a long stretch and that our invasion of Ray's space had to come to an end. It was proving difficult for Ray to concentrate on his work. He was beginning to grow irritable, and after my experience with Vincent, this was something I had little tolerance for and wished to avoid at all costs. For a short spell we rented a grimy, suffocating room above a shop. There was no ventilation, and the room trapped all the spicy cooking smells rising from the kitchen below. Curry has always been my favourite food with the exception of this period in time. Although the Indian landlord was kind to allow us to stay there in overcrowded conditions and eager to show me how to make certain dishes, he was also beginning to show signs of becoming amorous. As it was summer, I limited the time we spent there by going out as much as possible.

Within a month the house was ready for us to move into. I managed to move all our belongings from Ray's place by car making several journeys. Stupidly we wrangled over which of the two Christmas trees was mine until I capitulated leaving both trees behind undisturbed in his garden. Our new house was completely clean and needed no decorating at all. It was perfect for our needs. What luxury to have a decent house to ourselves complete with central heating, three bedrooms, and two reception rooms. What did it matter that it was less than a stone's throw from the railway track! It had a bathroom with an avocado suite! That ghastly shade of green was still quite popular at the time. Quickly we became well integrated in the neighbourhood as if we had already lived there for years, and I was very happy that I had clearly made the right decision to move back to London.

Meanwhile, Val and Dave had moved out to live in the country, and Tom and Cindy had already moved to Cornwall. Chris and family, who had taken in Suki when we had left Vincent, also moved from the flat across the road from our old house. Many years later I was shocked and saddened to hear that Chris had died. Clearly her health problems had been very serious.

By now I was beginning to feel that the bad times were certainly being overshadowed by good times, and we enjoyed a long period of stability. After years of moving from place to place, we could firmly drop anchor. For a while I developed a health problem. After all the physical exertion, I suffered from palpitations, which were quite alarming. The beating of my heart would race at high speed thumping inside my ribs as if it was trying to break out of its confinement. I discovered that bending over made it worse or triggered it, and only by lying flat on my back would the beating return to its normal rhythm. Every so often I would have to lie down in the staffroom at the school causing others concern. After seeing the doctor, I first wore an electronic heart-monitoring device for a few days. Then I was diagnosed with supraventricular tachycardia, a name I needed to rehearse before being able to pronounce it without hesitation. Finally a course of tablets resolved the problem, and I was reassured that it was not a serious condition.

From then on the Adams family values were to have fun and enjoy life. It was easy both for the children and for me to make friends with neighbouring families. Sometimes I would even join the kids outside in the street for a game of badminton.

Soon after we moved into the house, I took photos of the Sophie sitting on the front wall wearing her nurse's uniform but could not stop laughing as the wind kept blowing her headdress up making her look more like an archbishop. Whenever she dressed up in her clown costume, she would stuff tea towels down her legs to puff out the costume and walk stiffly around the house making us cry with laughter. She enjoyed sleepovers at her friend's and would often be seen carrying her duvet over her shoulder as she crossed the road. Although she claimed to be a vegetarian for a while and would reprimand me for eating fish, it soon transpired that at her friend's house she was enjoying chicken legs and slices of ham! As she was making exceptional progress at school, her teacher arranged for her to skip a year. I allowed her to have a guinea pig as her first pet. Before long we also adopted a pair of gerbils who rapidly multiplied to such an extent that I donated several to the science department at my school. The staff would crack constant jokes about the gerbils applying for jobs and involving themselves with the management of the school.

My friend who lived a few houses away had twin daughters who were young teenagers and always willing to babysit. Andy had friends next door, next door but one, and round the corner, so there was always someone knocking on the door. He loved riding his BMX bicycle up and down in the street and in the park. He was also content to play on his own, drawing and watching television. He was well behaved at school and made good, steady progress. Each summer he would always enjoy the challenge of the sponsored school fun run for charity and finish the run red-faced and sweating.

For a few years while Andy and Sophie shared a bedroom, I was able to take in a series of paying guests. First we enjoyed the company of a young German woman who worked as a language assistant at my school. Later on we had lodgers from Venezuela and Turkey. We enjoyed a couple of lovely camping holidays abroad. One summer we stopped off at campsites along the west coast of France and northern Spain. Another summer we spent touring north-eastern France and Switzerland. The children especially loved playing in the rivers, lakes, and swimming pools.

For Vincent, the access visits continued as before. Andy and Sophie enjoyed the family atmosphere and the regular opportunity to play with Lucy's children. I benefited from the free alternate weekends by having a break, carrying out minor home improvements, or catching up on my schoolwork. In the summer of 1994, while we looked after a French friend's flat, we visited Euro Disney and the main sights of the city. During our absence I had arranged to have some major work done at home. On the ground floor the two reception rooms and hall were made into an open plan area leaving the decorating for me to complete. Where a section of the fence had fallen down, I had a length of garden wall built. I even turned my hand to bricklaying to complete the remaining section. Though I managed to finish it, I found it a laborious task. My hands were small, each brick felt really heavy, and my skin would split and blister in places. Most of the decorating and regular maintenance work on the house I managed to do myself.

Before long Lucy and Vincent announced a new addition to their family, a baby daughter called Lisa—a half-sister to Andy and Sophie, who were six years and four years older respectively. Then, gradually over the next eighteen months, I began to notice signs that all was not well between Vincent and Lucy. First Vincent turned up on our doorstep with Bullet asking if I could take him. I was absolutely delighted to be reunited with him. Unlike Bailey, he was completely trustworthy around the children. But now he was overweight, and I had to put him on a strict diet.

Eventually Bullet lost his excess weight, but he still had his wandering spirit. When the children played out with their friends, we used to keep the door open allowing music from my new stereo system to drift into the street. Bullet had a habit of wandering down the street to sniff around and see what was going on. On more than one occasion, he even made his way on his own across two busy roads all the way to the park. Legend has it that he once bit a policeman's leg while the officer was trying to get hold of him. After that he became an instant hero back in the street. I doubt if this was true, as he had never shown aggression towards anyone before. Children would often come knocking at the door to tell me that Bullet was about to turn the corner at the end of the street, so I would have to drop everything and charge after him to bring him back home. Once, after we had searched everywhere for him, we were on the verge of giving up on him. After searching under my bed as I was sitting on the edge of the bed, I noticed the covers move. He had buried himself there and fallen asleep! Then one day he finally wandered off, sadly never ever to be seen again. Maybe he felt that he had to search for Vincent, or maybe he simply needed to go off exploring and satisfy his urge to wander freely. Maybe he went looking for food. Whatever the reason, we really missed him.

Vincent and Lucy must have been together for about four years when the turbulence in their relationship started to reach a serious stage. One weekend after I had dropped Andy and Sophie to stay at their house, Vincent brought them back only an hour or so later. The children told me that he had thrown a dish across the room in a fit of rage during a violent argument. It transpired that Vincent had become progressively hostile towards Lucy's older children. It was the same familiar story of accusations and suspicions based on his feelings of paranoia. Vincent's aggression towards Lucy's children must have been completely intolerable. Apparently he would pin them against the wall while he made accusations and threats. They must have been deeply traumatised.

Having had the benefit of hearing my testimony in court, Lucy realized that she had been taken in by his version of the breakdown of our marriage. Before the situation became too bad for her, she decided to leave him. Only by this time she was already pregnant with their next child. And so it happened that a second family now faced major disruption to their lives. This inevitably involved a series of changes of accommodation and schools together with all the heartache associated with another broken marriage.

Every few months Lucy and I would meet up together with all the children for mutual support. We both realized it was important for the children to continue to see each other regularly. Lucy appeared to take everything in her stride with a cheerful sense of resignation. After all, she had already experienced a marriage breakdown once before.

The new baby, John, was born a short while after she left home. He was two years younger than Lisa. Lucy was quite relaxed about Vincent having regular access to their two children and did not share my fears. They had separated before Vincent's condition grew much worse and protracted. Soon after their separation, Vincent started to phone me telling me that he felt there was nothing left to live for. He was clearly feeling suicidal, hanging by a thin thread. Though it seemed odd that he should turn to me of all people for support, I tried my best to offer him an opportunity to express his feelings. I offered encouragement, emphasising that this was a temporary phase that he would eventually find his way through.

Some time later he finally came to terms with the fact that Lucy had left him for good and did not bother me any longer with phone calls. When John was a few years old Vincent would occasionally visit us bringing the young children along. However he found it difficult to relate to Andy and Sophie, and his behaviour as a doting father to the two younger children showed a hurtful disregard for Andy's and Sophie's feelings. It had been a long time since he had paid the meagre amount of maintenance which the court had stipulated as a minimum. In fact he had only managed to pay this for about one or two years. Not that we depended on his contribution. It was less than the child benefit payments. I thought all along that he would have difficulty holding down a job.

One day he came round to our house alone with a hard luck story and asked if Andy and Sophie would return expensive gifts he had bought them, which made me feel really quite angry. I refused to let them hand back the gold chain and bracelet. On another occasion after this, he came round threatening to kick the door in, which naturally alarmed and unsettled all three of us.

By the time Sophie was old enough to start secondary school at the age of ten, we moved house. I never disclosed our new address or phone number to Vincent or had any further direct contact with him. This way, at least we hoped to enjoy some real security and peace of mind without fear of any unwelcome intrusion. Andy and Sophie had little interest in seeing their father, and he had clearly lost interest in them, becoming too self absorbed again. Weekly access visits by Lucy's children to Vincent still continued without any apparent detrimental effects. Vincent was no longer invited into their house, and before long Lucy's new partner moved in with her.

It was a good time for us to move house. Our new house was a couple of miles further away from the area where we had lived. It was much bigger with a front drive and longer rear garden, though I paid little more for it than the value of the house that we moved from. It had paid off to keep the old house well maintained. It was on the market for less than a week before I was able to accept a firm offer. I joked that the new house was big enough to put one child in the loft and the other in the cellar if they argued, as inevitably they did as they approached the turbulent teenage years. At least this house had no railway track behind it and no underground river flowing beneath it.

Over the years, I was able to pay for improvements to the neglected property. My career progressed further, so with more disposable income we enjoyed more holidays abroad including house swaps with families from Spain and France. Before moving house we even bought a new puppy and, some time later, a kitten. The dog was a cross-breed with a lovely temperament and long, soft fur. The kitten used to nestle in the dog's fur and suck his nipples making little squeaking sounds. It was as if the kitten was the dog's pet. When the cat was fully grown, he was very mischievous, but the dog would tell me about each of his antics, often taking the blame for his misdeeds by jumping up against me and offering a paw.

It took about twelve years to reach the stage in life where I felt that we had caught up in material terms with what we would have enjoyed if I had stayed in the marriage, though it is difficult to make the comparison. The satisfaction that I felt with my achievements was all the greater because I had struggled to do everything by myself without a partner. I felt that I was a stronger person as a result, as well as more able to show compassion after the ordeal I had been through with Vincent. It had certainly been a character-building exercise.

I am pleased that Andy and Sophie had had an opportunity to get to know their father for a few years as a family man in the security of his home with Lucy and her children. If, as adults, they should decide to look him up, that was fine by me. I just did not wish to take any risks while they were still growing up. Since they had now witnessed violent arguments between him and Lucy, they were able to see with their own eyes how irrational he could be and understand better how impossible it was to deal with him. They had no reason to fantasise about their father or to doubt my version of our family history.

Whenever people commented how difficult life must have been raising two children as a single parent, my reply was always unequivocal: 'It was not nearly as difficult as it was during my marriage to their father.'

Chapter 18

Reflections

When, as young teenagers, Andy and Sophie read my notes about my past life with Vincent and the circumstances of my leaving him, they had few questions and appeared to have no issues. I believe it paid off to tell them everything about our past, though it may have had an unsettling effect. Not only had they seen Vincent's disturbing behaviour when they spent weekends with him and Lucy, they have also seen enough other families to realize that ours is by no means unique in having a rocky past.

When she was old enough, Sophie decided that she wanted to visit her father from time to time. Vincent seemed pleased that she had taken the initiative to see him. At her request he agreed to do some work at her flat which involved some plumbing. However he showed reluctance and complained about a number of things, such as someone interfering with his tools. Once the work was completed, Sophie realized that offering him an opportunity to help her out involved a lot more than she was prepared to tolerate. On the other hand, Andy, after meeting him once or twice as a young adult, showed no further interest at all in seeing him again.

In January 2007 my father died suddenly at the age of ninety-three. My mother had died six years before him. Both my parents had long overcome their racist attitudes and showed great affection for their grandchildren. After my father found himself living alone he appreciated all the more the great value of family and we all became much closer, including my sister and her family. Only one week after the death of my father Sophie gave birth to her first child, a daughter. It was a highly emotional time. I was delighted to become a grandmother for the first time and looked forward to being closely involved in her young life. Sophie visited Vincent so that he could meet his baby granddaughter. By this time Lisa already had two young children, a son and a daughter, so Sophie's baby was not his first grandchild. Sophie remained good friends with her half-sister Lisa and eventually started to get to know John better as well. Andy joined in with their family gatherings too, so our early plan to keep the relationship alive between all four children paid off. Andy and John both enjoy playing an active role as uncles to their respective nieces and nephew. In August 2008, Sophie gave birth to a second daughter completing her lovely family. Andy still lives with me and we enjoy each other's company. Sophie and my granddaughters are frequent visitors helping to make ours a very close, supportive family.

All four of Vincent's children have grown up into well-adjusted adults. Andy and John each completed a university degree. Sophie qualified as a personal trainer, and Lisa as a beautician. I feel that it is unfair when people make sweeping statements and insinuations that single-parents families are somehow inferior. More thought should be given to the disadvantaged position of single parents without implying unfairly that deprivation leads to parental neglect or delinquency.

When the news reached us in the summer of 2007 that Vincent had died, it came as a complete shock to us all. In spite of his mental illness, he had always proclaimed himself to be invincible, a survivor with a strong fighting spirit. He was only sixty-six years old when he died. I had not seen him for several years and did not know that he had been ill. It had been his wish to keep his health problems confidential. I was told that he had undergone surgery on his abdomen but had not recovered from the operation. As he had continued to smoke all his life, I expect this had possibly contributed to his poor physical health. When we were married, he rarely used to eat breakfast, preferring several cups of coffee and cigarettes. During the acute phase of his illness, he had practically starved himself for several weeks due to his paranoia and obsessive behaviour.

I was pleased that Vincent had sustained a happy relationship with his youngest son, John, who was with him in hospital to the end and cared for him throughout his illness. John was the most favoured of his four children. Without his care Vincent would have died feeling alone and abandoned. I felt sad for the children that they had lost their father. For Sophie and Lisa, it was also sad that their children had lost a grandfather. For John it must have been a particularly difficult time, since they had been so close.

As for my own mixed feelings, the news of Vincent's death came mainly as a sense of release. From my own perspective, no longer could the prospect of unexpectedly bumping into him haunt me. No longer did I need to dread that he might discover where I live and make threats. Never again would I need to see his blazing eyes fire up as his temper exploded. Neither would I have to feel the shame of capitulating to his assaults. My recurrent dreams now occur less and less frequently. But the process of writing this has made me appreciate more fully that we had several happy years together in the early stages of our partnership, which understandably became overshadowed by the intensely traumatic times that followed.

While I would like to end my book with helpful facts and figures about schizophrenia, there could be a serious risk of misrepresentation in attempting to draw generalizations. All that I can be certain about is my experience of living with Vincent as an individual. In summary, Vincent managed to alienate those closest to him. It is quite clear to me that it was his mental illness that prevented him from forging long-term intimate relationships and fulfilling his cherished dream of enjoying a normal family life. Moreover, his failure to maintain such a relationship happened at least twice, once with me during my second pregnancy and then with Lucy during her second pregnancy, as well as possibly with April previously, though no children were involved in that relationship. This reduced capacity to form close relationships other than possibly with a child or parent is consistent with one of the main symptoms of schizophrenia, though this alone does not characterise the condition, of course. Several other symptoms must be evident in different settings before a definitive diagnosis can be reached by qualified psychiatrists.

One additional symptom is delusional beliefs, such as Vincent's idea that he was being affected by my ultrasound scans and by something which he believed I had had implanted inside my body. Some of his symptoms were far from clear-cut. For example, his paranoia was intertwined with excessive social anxiety and his feelings of being manipulated by others.

This was evident in his impressions both at work and at home as well as elsewhere. His belief that he was being followed while driving, that people would be waiting for him when he arrived at shops and at the hospital, as well as his belief that he was being watched by neighbours and passers-by were obvious examples of his paranoia. His sense of being manipulated was clear from his accusations against me as well as against Lucy's children at a later stage. His impression that he could not use certain tools at work and his annoyance at the parcel delivery man provide further examples of a related indicator, the belief that thoughts or feelings are being projected by others. Voices heard commenting on his work on the house and the strange 'ee ee' and 'la la' language which he claimed to hear were yet more examples of symptoms. Add to these symptoms his loss of motivation, his aggression, his lack of close friends, his self-absorbed attitude as well as an inability to empathise and there remains no doubt in my mind that he struggled with a catalogue of serious psychological disorders, no matter what label is assigned to them in summary.

As for the tragic outcome of my marriage to Vincent, I firmly believe that this was due to the collective failure to get him the treatment and medication that he badly needed. This was the collective responsibility of medical professionals, social services, and the police together with legal procedures, all of which were sadly inadequate. The lack of accessible guidance and support for me as his closest relative and sole carer were also sadly lacking. Not only this, but my attempts to report to the police and certain medical professionals the serious state of his symptoms more than once fell on deaf ears with little regard for my own distress. I acknowledge that the health professionals were bound by the legal procedures at that time and that Vincent was altogether capable of masking his symptoms, coming across as being of sound mind on occasions.

If Vincent had received the correct treatment promptly, our story would surely have ended very differently. However I also acknowledge that there is still no guarantee that Vincent would have ever consented to treatment or committed to a sustained course of treatment over the long term. If he had carried out his threats of suicide, as I feel sure many sufferers of schizophrenia do, then who, if anyone, would have been held to account?

With regard to his aggression and violent outbursts, there is also little doubt in my mind that these were precipitated by his illness, though there is limited concrete evidence to support this. It is possible that his violent tendencies were rooted in his early conditioning. As a child he had been beaten by his father. Domestic abuse is still a huge issue in society as a whole. From what I have read and been told about the incidence of violence, it is only a small proportion of those suffering from paranoid schizophrenia who react in this way. It is reported that in any one year 8 per cent of patients diagnosed with schizophrenia will commit an act of violence compared to approximately 2 per cent of people who are not diagnosed. The incidence rises to 30 per cent in the case of those diagnosed with schizophrenia who also have issues with drugs or alcohol. By his own admission, Vincent had smoked cannabis but never smoked since I met him, having given up well before we had met. Patients who do commit acts of violence are deemed to do so without awareness that their actions are wrong, as they are suffering from a disease of the mind and therefore are subject to diminished responsibility.

All I know is that, in our first few years together, there was no sign of overt violence in the way that Vincent behaved towards me. He changed from a devoted, loving partner into a controlling bully, giving me no alternative but to respond with the stealth of a secret agent. As he became acutely ill, the way that his paranoia centred on me was incontrovertible, unwavering, and positively terrifying. It made absolutely no difference to him that I was pregnant and highly vulnerable. I shudder to think how Lucy's children must have felt when Vincent's paranoia centred on them.

It is estimated that in the United Kingdom one in four people will suffer from mental health problems at some stage in their lives. Recent public information on domestic abuse points out the equally staggering statistics that one in four women experience domestic abuse compared to one in six men. Domestic abuse includes those in same sex relationships and is carried out by people of all races, ages, religions, and backgrounds. The information emphasises clearly that it is not the fault of the victim and makes the point that no one deserves abuse. Abuse is not acceptable. Examples of domestic abuse include threats, verbal and emotional abuse, financial control, neglect, and the imposition of constraints. Domestic violence can worsen over time. As if this were not bad enough, abuse can be especially intense during a partner's pregnancy and after the birth of a child.

Naturally curious about possible causes in terms of biological and environmental factors surrounding schizophrenia, I searched for evidence. I acknowledge that I am no scientific expert in psychology and that there are serious risks of misrepresenting facts, in particular concerning schizophrenia, which is a highly complex disorder. Understanding of the condition is also subject to change in the light of ongoing research. Readers should refer to primary sources of information written by specialists in the field. However, I would like to share a certain level of basic knowledge based on reported evidence. Since carers and families play a crucial role in supporting sufferers, it is obvious to me that as much information as possible should be shared.

Research into the possible causes of schizophrenia has given rise to various theories focusing on biological factors. It appears that patients with schizophrenia have reduced blood flow in the frontal regions of the brain and reduced activity in the frontal lobes. Theories that the cause may be a virus have been explored. These include research examining associations between the incidence of schizophrenia and factors affecting the pregnancy of patients' mothers, in particular winter births, influenza during mid pregnancy, and poor diet during early pregnancy. Hormonal differences between male and female patients have also been researched, since the average age of the onset of schizophrenia is reported to occur about five years earlier in females than in males.

Environmental factors are strongly associated with traumatic emotional events. It appears to be firmly established that there is a strong correlation between psychosis and psychological stress and that symptoms become more and more acute with further stresses. I was unable to pinpoint any single traumatic event as an early trigger leading to Vincent's acute episode. I can only surmise that, in his case, it was an accumulation of stresses: the pressure to complete the work on the house, the birth of our second child, and the stress of returning to work for an employer. It is also quite possible that cannabis use in his earlier life had played a part in triggering his original psychosis, though this is speculation. If this is the case, it presents a potentially strong basis for assuming permanent damage to mental health for anyone susceptible.

With regard to patients' entitlement to refuse treatment for schizophrenia, in most cases doctors would recommend disregarding their decision on the basis that the condition to be treated itself causes impaired judgement. However, if the sufferer's view is persistent after all the advantages and disadvantages of treatment have been explained, it is possible in some circumstances for doctors to respect their wishes to reject treatment. Following treatment, not all patients accept that the treatment helped them. Therefore the whole issue of accessing and evaluating treatment is fraught with difficulties.

I understand and accept that, with the 1983 Mental Health Act in the United Kingdom, there have been many improvements in provision for people with mental health problems. It is unfortunate that our family so narrowly missed benefiting from the revised legal procedures as well as the new provision of specialist police units and other services and areas of support. Significantly among the changes, the revised Mental Health Act authorises the closest relative to be involved in the forced admission procedures. There is also much greater emphasis on listening to carers and on creating a general climate of care. Clearly this would have made a difference in the case of Vincent's prospects of accessing treatment, assuming that the revised procedures are implemented in a rigorous and consistent way.

I hope that, in spite of economic difficulties and austerity measures, such improvements in the provision of services can be sustained and further developed. The consequences of any potential lapses in services would be disastrous with far-reaching ramifications for sufferers and their families, as my own story clearly demonstrates. The human cost of such lapses would be too great to contemplate.

As Vincent's wife and the mother of two of his children, I was able to leave home, take advantage of divorce proceedings, and start a new life. So was Lucy. We were able to relinquish all responsibility for him in the interests of raising our families. For some family members these options are simply not available. For a parent or a child of a mentally ill person, the burden of responsibility may be a lifelong commitment with little relief.

I was fortunate to come across many people who showed me help and kindness when I was in utter desperation, distress and despair. People acted spontaneously out of sheer goodwill and compassion. Without the help and support of these people, I would have been at a complete loss, and our fate as a family would have been even more precarious. My thanks to you all.

Sufferers and their families have to face social stigma towards mental illness, which is deeply rooted in our history and culture. Lack of understanding adds to fear of mental illness and lack of empathy for sufferers. In the case of schizophrenia, because it is such a complicated disorder, it is not surprising that there are common misconceptions. Even diagnosis by specialists in the field is a protracted and uncertain business. By reducing and eliminating social stigma, we can hope to minimise sufferers' own poor self-image, resistance to diagnosis, and rejection of treatment. Then maybe they would stand a better chance of gaining some measure of insight into their own condition and feel more accepting of help and treatment, which is so often the first hurdle to overcome. In Vincent's case, as far as I am aware, this first hurdle was never crossed.

References

Frith, Christopher and Eve Johnstone. 2003. *Schizophrenia: A Very Short Introduction*. Oxford: Oxford University Press.

Recommended further reading

Elyn R. Saks. 2008. The Centre Cannot Hold: A Memoir of My Schizophrenia. Hyperion Books

Helpful sources of information in the UK

Mental health

www.mind.org.uk
www.turn2me.org
www.grayhealthcare.co.uk
www.penrose.org.uk
www.youngminds.org.uk www.greatbritishcommunity.org

Domestic Abuse

www.onespace.org.uk/abuse
www.womensaid.org.uk
www.victimsupport.org.uk
www.refuge.org.uk
www.nationaldomesticviolencehelpline.org.uk
Freephone 24 hour helpline: 08082000247

Suggested Book Club Questions

1. To what extent, if any, do you believe that people suffering from serious mental illness such as paranoid schizophrenia should be entitled to reject treatment?

2. On what grounds, if any, do you think that Nicki was justified in trying to get Vincent admitted to hospital for treatment?

3. Should Nicki have left Vincent earlier? If so, at what point?

4. What do you think are serious implications for cannabis users given that there is evidence that cannabis use can lead to psychosis?

5. What role, if any, do you consider that racist attitudes may have played a part in the way that events developed in this story?

6. How do you think that gender discrimination may have affected Nicki?

7. What potential adverse effects might impact babies and young children who witness marital conflict, violence, and other forms of abuse?

8. How important do you think it is for children to maintain contact with half-brothers and / or half-sisters?

9. In what ways do you think that social stigma against mental illness can be reduced or eradicated?

10. Who do you think should accept the ultimate responsibility for Vincent's lack of treatment?

11. What are your views on care in the community as distinct from hospital care?

12. How significant do you think Vincent's upbringing was in precipitating his illness?

Printed in the United States
By Bookmasters